Reading Achievement
Comprehension Activities to Promote Essential Reading Skills

Grade 2

D1530055

by
Meadow Bond

Table of Contents

Introduction

Welcome to the **Reading Achievement** series! Each book in this series is designed to reinforce the reading skills appropriate for each grade level and to encourage high-level thinking skills. Because reading is an essential part of all disciplines, mastery of these skills can help students succeed in all academic areas. In addition, experiencing success in reading can increase a student's self-esteem and motivate him or her to read more, both in and out of the classroom.

Each **Reading Achievement** book offers challenging questions for students to answer in response to a variety of grade-level appropriate passages. Various types of reading passages are represented in this book, including fiction, nonfiction, charts and graphs, and word searches. The format and questions are similar to those found on standardized reading tests. The experience students gain from answering questions in this format may help increase their test scores. In addition, these exercises can be used to enhance your school-adopted reading program, to individualize instruction, to provide extra practice for home schoolers, or to review skills between grades.

The following reading skills are covered within this book:

- **cause and effect**
- **comprehension**
- **critical thinking**
- **fact or opinion**
- **following directions**
- **main ideas/details**
- **reference skills**
- **sequencing**
- **true or false**
- **vocabulary**

Each **Reading Achievement** book contains additional features to enhance usability. Four pretests, in standardized test format, have been included at the beginning of each book. The pretests have been designed so that they may be used individually, as four stand-alone tests, or in groups. Another convenient feature is a scoring box on each activity page. This scoring box can be programmed to suit your specific classroom and student needs with total problems, total correct, and score.

Read the story below.

A little fawn walked through the woods. He was lost and looking for his mother. He sniffed the air and the grass. He heard water in the brook and wind in the trees, but he couldn't hear his mother. He was afraid.

The fawn began to run through the forest. Soon he saw a large doe near the brook. It was his mother! He ran to her and rubbed his nose against her side. He was not afraid any more.

_____

Read the question and circle the letter beside the correct answer.

1. This story is about _____.
   A. a lost fawn   B. a lost bobcat   C. a storm   D. mothers

2. Which word rhymes with "fawn" and "dawn"?
   A. down   B. some   C. lawn   D. came

3. In this story, a "doe" is a _____.
   A. mother deer   B. mother fox   C. baby   D. daddy

4. The word "sniffed" means _____.
   A. tasted   B. smelled   C. touched   D. saw

5. A "brook" is the same as a _____.
   A. meadow   B. creek   C. field   D. sea

Total Problems:	Total Correct:	Score:

Read the story below.

Once in Greece lived a slave named Aesop. He was a good storyteller. He was so good that his master set him free. He traveled from place to place telling stories. Later his stories were put in a book called *Aesop's Fables.*

The fables are short and most tell about animals. The animals talk and act like people. Each fable tells about the good and bad things that people do. At the end of each fable is a moral, or lesson, that tells people how they should live. One of the morals taken from a fable is "Slow and steady wins the race."

Read the question and circle the letter beside the correct answer.

1. This story is about a slave named _____.
    A. Greece   B. Fable   C. Moral   D. Aesop

2. In this story the word "fable" means _____.
    A. slave   B. moral   C. rule   D. story

3. Why did Aesop's master set him free?
    A. He was handsome.   B. He told good stories.
    C. He needed to go home.   D. He felt sorry for him.

4. In this story the word "moral" means the same as _____.
    A. lesson   B. story   C. fable   D. animal

Read the story below.

People who never throw anything away are often called "pack rats". That name comes from a real animal with the same name. It is a rat no bigger than your hand, but it builds a huge home. Pack rats like to carry bright and shiny objects to their homes. They always leave something to pay for what they take. They may leave jewelry, or some other shiny treasure. Pack rats never stop building. Eyeglasses and mirrors have been found built into the walls of their homes. It is unclear why pack rats take objects for their homes, but it is thought that they want their homes to look pretty.

_____

Read the question and circle the letter beside the correct answer.

1. This story is about _____.
   - A. people called pack rats
   - B. rats called pack rats
   - C. how to make a pretty home
   - D. jewelry and treasure

2. What kind of objects do pack rats like to take to their homes?
   - A. food
   - B. broken objects
   - C. bright, shiny objects
   - D. expensive objects

3. How do pack rats pay for what they take?
   - A. They work to pay it off.
   - B. No one knows for sure.
   - C. They leave some other treasure.
   - D. They pay with money.

Total Problems: _____   Total Correct: _____   Score: _____

Name _____

Read each story. Then, answer the question that follows.

Dogs do funny things. For example, when they get wet, they wait until people are standing right beside them, and then they shake water on them! It is not known why they do that. Some people say that it is because they do not like being wet, and that is their way of showing it. Another idea is that they are having so much fun that they want to share it.

1. This story is about _____.
   - A. dogs shaking water
   - B. giving a dog a bath
   - C. ways to stay dry
   - D. bad dogs

Duncan and his family went to the beach. They played in the sand and built sand castles. They swam in the ocean and played in the waves. They walked along the beach and collected seashells. When it was time to come back home, they were sad to leave the seaside.

2. This story is about _____.
   - A. how to build a sand castle
   - B. salt water
   - C. Duncan's family at the beach
   - D. collecting seashells

Name _____ Pretest

Read the story below.

A little fawn walked through the woods. He was lost and looking for his mother. He sniffed the air and the grass. He heard water in the brook and wind in the trees, but he couldn't hear his mother. He was afraid.

The fawn began to run through the forest. Soon he saw a large doe near the brook. It was his mother! He ran to her and rubbed his nose against her side. He was not afraid any more.

Read the question and circle the letter beside the correct answer.

1. This story is about _____.
   (A) a lost fawn   B. a lost bobcat   C. a storm   D. mothers

2. Which word rhymes with "fawn" and "dawn"?
   A. down   B. some   (C) lawn   D. came

3. In this story, a "doe" is a _____.
   (A) mother deer   B. mother fox   C. baby   D. daddy

4. The word "sniffed" means _____.
   A. tasted   (B) smelled   C. touched   D. saw

5. A "brook" is the same as a _____.
   A. meadow   (B) creek   C. field   D. sea

4 | Total Problems: | Total Correct: | Score: | © Carson-Dellosa CD-2201

Name _____ Pretest

Read the story below.

Once in Greece lived a slave named Aesop. He was a good storyteller. He was so good that his master set him free. He traveled from place to place telling stories. Later his stories were put in a book called *Aesop's Fables*.

The fables are short and most tell about animals. The animals talk and act like people. Each fable tells about the good and bad things that people do. At the end of each fable is a moral, or lesson, that tells people how they should live. One of the morals taken from a fable is "Slow and steady wins the race."

Read the question and circle the letter beside the correct answer.

1. This story is about a slave named _____.
   A. Greece   B. Fable   C. Moral   (D) Aesop

2. In this story the word "fable" means _____.
   A. slave   B. moral   C. rule   (D) story

3. Why did Aesop's master set him free?
   A. He was handsome.   (B) He told good stories.
   C. He needed to go home.   D. He felt sorry for him.

4. In this story the word "moral" means the same as _____.
   (A) lesson   B. story   C. fable   D. animal

© Carson-Dellosa CD-2201 | Total Problems: | Total Correct: | Score: | 5

Name _____ Pretest

Read the story below.

People who never throw anything away are often called "pack rats". That name comes from a real animal with the same name. It is a rat no bigger than your hand, but it builds a huge home. Pack rats like to carry bright and shiny objects to their homes. They always leave something to pay for what they take. They may leave jewelry, or some other shiny treasure. Pack rats never stop building. Eyeglasses and mirrors have been found built into the walls of their homes. It is unclear why pack rats take objects for their homes, but it is thought that they want their homes to look pretty.

Read the question and circle the letter beside the correct answer.

1. This story is about _____.
   A. people called pack rats   (B) rats called pack rats
   C. how to make a pretty home   D. jewelry and treasure

2. What kind of objects do pack rats like to take to their homes?
   A. food   B. broken objects
   (C) bright, shiny objects   D. expensive objects

3. How do pack rats pay for what they take?
   A. They work to pay it off.   B. No one knows for sure.
   (C) They leave some other treasure.   D. They pay with money.

6 | Total Problems: | Total Correct: | Score: | © Carson-Dellosa CD-2201

Name _____ Pretest

Read each story. Then, answer the question that follows.

Dogs do funny things. For example, when they get wet, they wait until people are standing right beside them, and then they shake water on them! It is not known why they do that. Some people say that it is because they do not like being wet, and that is their way of showing it. Another idea is that they are having so much fun that they want to share it.

1. This story is about _____.
   (A) dogs shaking water   B. giving a dog a bath
   C. ways to stay dry   D. bad dogs

Duncan and his family went to the beach. They played in the sand and built sand castles. They swam in the ocean and played in the waves. They walked along the beach and collected seashells. When it was time to come back home, they were sad to leave the seaside.

2. This story is about _____.
   A. how to build a sand castle   B. salt water
   (C) Duncan's family at the beach   D. collecting seashells

© Carson-Dellosa CD-2201 | Total Problems: | Total Correct: | Score: | 7

Name _____

Follow the directions for each picture.

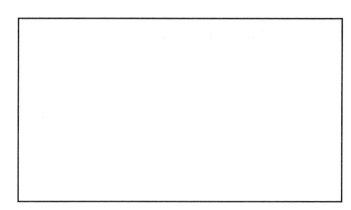

1. Draw a tail on the dog.
2. Draw black spots on the dog.
3. Make up a name for the dog and write it under the picture.
4. Give the dog a red collar.

1. Draw a large green circle in the box.
2. Draw three yellow triangles inside the circle.
3. Connect the three triangles with blue lines.
4. Trace the box with orange.

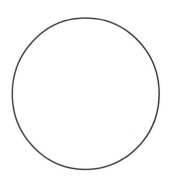

1. Draw a smile, a nose, and two green eyes in the circle.
2. Give the face curly red hair.
3. Draw freckles on the face.
4. Draw a blue box around the face.

1. Put an X on the smallest mouse.
2. Color the largest mouse pink.
3. Put dots under the two smallest mice.
4. Draw a line above the mice.

Total Problems:	Total Correct:	Score:

Follow the directions for each picture.

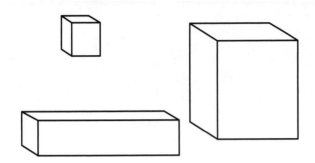

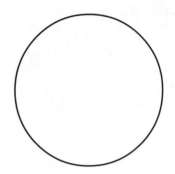

1. Draw bows on the boxes.
2. Color the smallest box red.
3. Color the longest box blue.
4. Color the largest box green.

1. Draw a line from the top to the bottom of the circle.
2. Draw yellow and green stripes in the right half of the circle.
3. Draw purple spots on the left.
4. Draw red lines coming out of the circle.

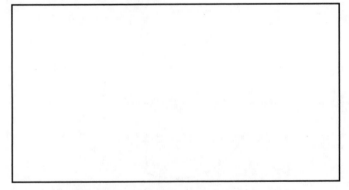

1. Draw a pig on the left side of the barn.
2. Color the barn red.
3. Draw two clouds and a sun in the sky.
4. Draw green grass on the ground.

1. Write your last name inside the box in black.
2. Trace the first letter with red.
3. Trace the last letter with blue.
4. Circle all of the vowels.

Total Problems: **Total Correct:**   **Score:**

Follow the directions to create the picture.

1. Draw a picture of a house in the middle of the box.
2. Draw a little girl on the right side of the house and a little boy on the left side of the house.
3. Put a green bow in the little girl's hair.
4. Give the boy red shoes.
5. Draw a sun in the top left corner of the box.
6. Draw a sidewalk in front of the house.
7. Draw a dog beside the little boy.

Read the story below.

   Tina and Timmy are twins. They are eight years old.
Tina and Timmy both have red hair, but Tina's hair is
long and Timmy's hair is short. Tina wears her hair in
braids. Both twins have freckles, but their eye color is
different. Timmy's eyes are blue, and Tina's are green.
Tina smiles a lot. She is missing her two front teeth.
Timmy is not missing any teeth, but he just got braces.
Tina and Timmy have a lot of similarities and differences.

Write the answer to the questions on the lines provided.

1. What is the main idea of the paragraph?

_____

_____

2. What are some things that are the same about Tina and Timmy?

_____

_____

3. What are some things that are different about Tina and Timmy?

_____

_____

_____

Total Problems: _____   Total Correct: _____   Score: _____

Find the words from the word box in the word search puzzle below. Circle the words you find.

Tina and Timmy Word Search

```
F  T  E  E  T  H  D  S
G  R  C  Q  M  E  E  S
R  B  E  W  R  C  T  M
E  L  V  C  A  K  W  I
E  U  E  R  K  L  I  L
N  E  B  V  T  L  N  E
S  H  O  R  T  J  E  B
D  B  R  A  I  D  S  S
```

Word Box				
blue	braids	green	short	teeth
braces	freckles	red	smile	twin

Total Problems:	Total Correct:	Score:

Read the story below.

When Mom and Dad go out, Arden and Kate have a babysitter. The first time Chris babysat, the girls were nervous. "What if he isn't nice?" said Arden. "Don't worry," Mom said. "I'm sure he will be a great sitter."

When Chris got there the girls were playing checkers. "What do you want for dinner?" Chris asked. Both girls said, "Pizza!" at the same time. "What toppings do you like?" asked Chris. "I like pepperoni and mushrooms," said Kate. "I like green pepper and sausage," Arden said. Chris liked his pizza with plain cheese. "Looks like we have a problem," said Chris.

"I have an idea," Kate said. "Instead of ordering pizza, we could make one. That way we could put whatever toppings we want on our share." "What a good idea," said Arden. "Or, we could each make our own pizza." "You girls are smart," said Chris. The three of them went down to the kitchen and made pizzas for dinner. Before they knew it, Mom and Dad were home. "Did you have fun?" asked Dad. "Yes!" said Arden. "When can Chris babysit again?"

Name _____

Pizza for Dinner

Complete the following activities. Write the answer on the lines provided where appropriate.

1. What is the problem in the story?

_____

_____

2. How did Chris and the girls solve the problem?

_____

_____

_____

3. What are some other ways the problem could have been solved?

_____

_____

_____

4. Draw a picture of each person's pizza below.

Arden's Pizza   **Kate's Pizza**   **Chris' Pizza**

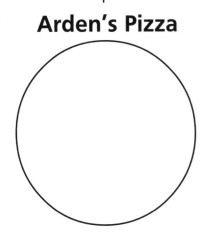 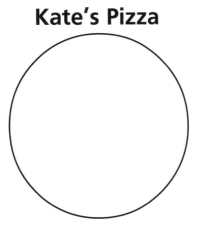 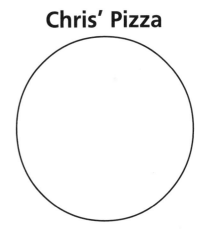

Total Problems:	Total Correct:	Score:

15

© Carson-Dellosa CD-2201

Read the story below.

   Max loves to go to the park. If it is sunny outside Max's owner, Allison, takes him to the park after school. The first thing Max does when he gets to the park is chase the other dogs. After a fun game of chase, Max swims in the creek. Allison likes it when Max goes for a swim because it washes some of the dirt off of his white coat. Then, Max takes a nap under the picnic table before he and Allison go back home.

Complete the following activities. Write the answer on the lines provided where appropriate.

1. Number the sentences 1–3 in the order they happen in the story.

   _____ Max goes for a swim.

   _____ Max chases other dogs.

   _____ Max takes a nap.

2. Color the bone that tells the main idea of the story green. Color the other bones blue.

   Max chases other dogs.   Swimming is fun.

   Max loves to go to the park.   Max takes a nap.

Total Problems: _____   Total Correct: _____   Score: _____

Name _____

Find the words from the word box in the word search puzzle below. Circle the words you find.

A Dog's Day Word Search

```
T  A  B  L  E  K  C  E  W
M  W  M  X  R  C  S  L  X
D  H  C  A  I  A  H  O  R
W  Q  P  N  H  M  Z  S  Q
B  A  C  C  N  B  Z  U  C
D  I  S  C  S  B  R  N  R
P  N  Z  H  O  W  F  N  E
N  A  H  C  E  A  I  Y  E
W  H  I  T  E  S  T  M  K
```

Word Box

chase	creek	picnic	swim	washes
coat	park	sunny	table	white

Total Problems:	Total Correct:	Score:

17

Read the story below.

Mother sent Bunny to the patch to gather carrots. Bunny picked them quickly because it had started snowing, and it was getting cold. She was on her way home from the carrot patch when she realized she was lost.

She tried to go back to the big oak tree to look for her tracks, but the snow had covered them. Then she hopped to the top of a hill to look for her home, but it was no use. Bunny had just about given up when she saw her friend, Owl. Owl told Bunny she could warm up in his house until the snow stopped.

Owl was happy to have a visitor. He welcomed Bunny and offered her a cup of tea. After Bunny had warmed up and visited a while, Owl made a suggestion. He told Bunny that he could fly above her as she hopped to lead her home. Owl explained to Bunny that it was easier to see a long way from the sky.

Owl guided Bunny home where Mother was waiting. The carrots were a delicious addition to the pot of stew that Mother had been making. To thank him for his help, Bunny's family invited Owl to stay for dinner.

Name _____

Complete the following activities. Write the answer on the lines provided where appropriate.

1. Why couldn't Bunny find her way home?

_____

_____

_____

2. How did Owl help Bunny?

_____

_____

_____

3. Number the sentences 1 – 5 in the order they happen in the story.

   _____ Bunny realized that she was lost.

   _____ Mother sent Bunny to the carrot patch to get carrots.

   _____ Bunny and Owl had tea and visited.

   _____ Bunny went back to the oak tree to look for her tracks.

   _____ Owl joined Bunny's family for stew.

Total Problems:	Total Correct:	Score:

Read the story below.

Leonard Lion wanted to be a security guard at the bank. When he applied for the job, everyone laughed. They said, "Leonard, you are too small and nice to be a security guard." Leonard was sad.

Leonard was on his way home when he heard crying coming from a pile of leaves. He went closer to take a look and found Miranda Mouse. She was hiding behind a leaf. "What's wrong Miranda?" he asked.

"Mrs. Nimble, who works at the daycare, has to move away. Now there is no one to watch our children."

"I'm sorry Miranda. It sounds like we are both having a bad day. I didn't get the job at the bank, and you are worried about who will watch your children."

"I have an idea," said Miranda. "You are great with children, and it sounds like you need a job. What do you think about working at the daycare?"

"Well," said Leonard, "I'll try it and see how it goes."

Leonard loved working in the daycare, and the children loved Leonard. He read stories, gave out hugs, and painted with the children. Leonard never worried about not being big or tough again.

Complete the following activities. Write the answer on the lines provided where appropriate.

1. What was Leonard's problem?

_____

_____

2. What was Miranda's problem?

_____

_____

3. How are the problems solved?

_____

_____

4. Draw lines to connect Leonard to the words that tell about him. Draw lines to connect Miranda to things that tell about her. Some phrases may connect to both characters.

- wants to be a bank guard

- worried about the children

- is having a bad day

- has a new job

Name _____

Read the story below.

Tootsie was a healthy dog. Mom made sure she stayed healthy by taking her to the veterinarian for a check up once a year. When it was time to go to the vet, Tootsie was scared.

Mom put Tootsie in the car. Tootsie tried to wiggle out of Mom's arms. "Don't worry Tootsie. Dr. Winn is a nice vet. You will like her." Tootsie was still scared.

When they got to the vet's office Tootsie started shaking. Mom picked her up and took her into the office. "Hello Tootsie!" said a pretty lady behind the desk. "Do you want a treat?" Tootsie perked her ears. She wagged her tail when the nice lady took a treat out of the jar.

They waited in the waiting room until Dr. Winn called them. "Hi there Tootsie," Dr. Winn said. She showed Mom and Tootsie to a little room. Dr. Winn talked to Tootsie the whole time that she gave her a check up. Soon, Dr. Winn was putting Tootsie back on the floor and giving her another treat. "Well, Tootsie looks great," Dr. Winn said to Mom. "We will see you in a year."

22

Complete the following activities. Write the answer on the lines provided where appropriate.

1. Number the sentences 1-4 in the order they happen in the story.

   _____ The lady at the front desk was nice to Tootsie.

   _____ Tootsie was not afraid to go to the vet anymore.

   _____ Mom and Tootsie met Dr. Winn.

   _____ Tootsie was afraid to go to the vet.

2. How did Mom make sure Tootsie stayed healthy?

   _____

   _____

3. What does the word "veterinarian" mean?

   _____

   _____

4. Why do you think Tootsie was afraid to go to the vet?

   _____

   _____

   _____

Read the story below.

   Darby enjoyed helping her dad rake leaves. Her favorite part was jumping in the biggest pile after the raking was done. The leaves were like a cloud on the ground.

   One day, as Dad was taking a lunch break, Darby decided to take a break too. She plopped down on the biggest leaf pile to rest. Darby was startled when she heard a little voice next to her ear. She looked over to see an inchworm on top of a leaf.

   "I was wondering if you could do me a favor," said the inchworm. "Earlier, I was crawling across a leaf up in that tree, and the leaf fell off while I was on it. It would take me all day to climb back up to the branch I was on. I was wondering if you would let me sit on the end of your rake. If you held the rake up to the tree, it would give me a big head start." Darby agreed to help.

   When Dad came back outside, he and Darby finished the yard. Just before Darby went inside to clean up, she turned and looked at the tree where she had taken her new friend. She was glad she had helped him get home.

Complete the following activities. Write the answer on the lines provided where appropriate.

1. What was the inchworm's problem?

_____

_____

_____

2. Read each sentence. If it is something that could happen in real life, write "realistic." If it is something make believe, write "fantasy."

   Darby helps her father rake the yard.   _____

   An inchworm talks to a little girl.   _____

   An inchworm falls from a tree.   _____

   Dad takes a break for lunch.   _____

3. Number the sentences 1–4 in the order they happen in the story.

   _____ Darby helped the inchworm.

   _____ Darby helped Dad finish raking the leaves.

   _____ An inchworm said hello to Darby.

   ——— Dad took a lunch break.

Total Problems: _____   Total Correct: _____   Score: _____

Name _____

Read the story below.

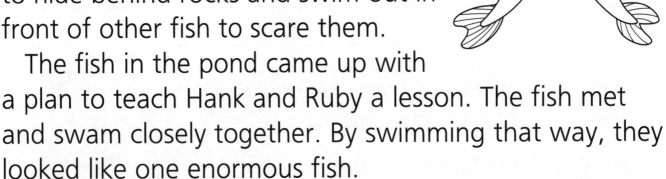

   Hank and Ruby were fish who lived in a pond. They loved to play tricks on other fish. Hank and Ruby liked to hide behind rocks and swim out in front of other fish to scare them.

   The fish in the pond came up with a plan to teach Hank and Ruby a lesson. The fish met and swam closely together. By swimming that way, they looked like one enormous fish.

   First they passed Ruby. She was hiding behind a plant waiting to scare someone. When she peeked out to see how close they were, Ruby was so frightened that she swam rapidly in the other direction.

   Hank heard Ruby coming and thought that she was going to play a joke on him. He hid behind a rock and waited. When he heard her get closer, he jumped out. He came face to face with Ruby and with what looked like the world's largest fish! Hank and Ruby were terrified. They had never seen a fish so big. They swam away. Hank and Ruby were very careful from then on. No one ever told them that they had been tricked, but neither Hank nor Ruby tried to scare another fish again.

Complete the following activities. Write the answer on the lines provided where appropriate.

1. Who are the main characters in the story?

_____

2. What is the setting of the story?

_____

_____

3. How did Hank and Ruby scare the other fish?

_____

_____

4. Why did Hank and Ruby stop scaring the other fish?

_____

_____

5. Use context clues to find the meaning of the following words.

   frighten   _____

   terrified   _____

   enormous   _____

   rapidly   _____

   peeked   _____

Total Problems:	Total Correct:	Score:

Read the story below.

John's scout group was going camping. He had a lot to do to get ready. He knew it was important to check his camping equipment to make sure everything worked. John laid his sleeping bag, tent, and cooking set on his bed, and his dad helped him inspect it.

Next, John went to the kitchen. John made trail mix in case he got hungry while hiking. He put peanuts, raisins, and chocolate chips in a plastic bag and shook it.

The next morning John's dad drove him to meet the other scouts. The leader helped them load their equipment into the truck. After driving an hour they arrived.

When they got there, everyone put on their backpacks and hiked toward the campsite. They stopped for a break after a while and had a snack. Everyone agreed that John's trail mix was delicious.

After their snack, the boys finished the hike to camp. When they arrived, they pitched their tents, collected firewood, and cleaned the campsite. The scout leader built a fire and they roasted hot dogs and marshmallows. They ended the day telling stories by the campfire.

Complete the following activities. Write the answer on the lines provided where appropriate.

1. Number the sentences 1–4 in the order they happen in the story.

   _____ John shared his trail mix.

   _____ Dad drove John to meet the others.

   _____ Stories were told by the campfire.

   _____ The boys set up camp.

2. According to the story, how do you make trail mix?

   _____

   _____

3. Which word from the story means the same as the given definition?

   checking to make sure something works   _____

   following a trail through the woods   _____

   spending the night in the woods   _____

   putting up a tent   _____

Total Problems:	Total Correct:	Score:

Read the story below.

Helena Horsefly was a hard worker. She had never had a vacation. So, one day she decided to go to Mexico.

The first thing she did when she arrived was eat dinner. On her way out of the restaurant, she noticed that the man at the next table had forgotten his wallet. "I should return this," thought Helena. She took it to the address on the driver's license, which turned out to be a mansion. Helena knocked and waited. Finally, a handsome frog came to the door.

"I'm sorry to trouble you," Helena said, "but a man left his wallet where I was dining. This is the address on his license, so I thought I would return it. "

"That's my doorman Alfred's wallet," said the frog. "He is off tonight. I am Señor Frog."

"I am pleased to meet you," said Helena. Señor Frog invited Helena to come inside. After that night they spent a lot of time together and eventually fell in love. They decided to get married. Helena quit her job and moved to Mexico. She was so glad that she had decided to take a vacation.

Name _____

Complete the following activities. Write the answer on the lines provided where appropriate.

1. Why did Helena go to Señor Frog's house?

_____

_____

_____

2. What happened when Helena got to Señor Frog's house?

_____

_____

_____

3. Who is Alfred?

_____

_____

4. Number the sentences 1–4 in the order they happen in the story.

_____ Señor Frog introduced himself to Helena.

_____ Helena and Señor Frog got married.

_____ Helena went to Mexico.

_____ Helena found a wallet.

Total Problems:	Total Correct:	Score:

Read the story below.

Latisha, Hope, and Valeria decided to build sand castles. Latisha made a castle by letting wet sand drip between her fingers. When she was finished, her castle had two pointed towers.

Hope used a bucket to make her castle. She put two buckets of sand side by side and put a third bucket on top. Her castle looked like a pyramid.

Valeria's castle was square. She collected shells and seaweed from the beach to decorate her castle. She used her fingers to add square windows on the sides.

All of the castles were beautiful. The girls laughed as the waves knocked down their castles. They knew that tomorrow they could build some new ones.

Fill in the circle beside the correct answer.

1. How many towers did Latisha's castle have?
   ○ four   ○ two   ○ one

2. What did Hope's castle look like when it was finished?
   ○ a pyramid   ○ a box   ○ a seashell

3. What was the shape of Valeria's castle?
   ○ circle   ○ triangle   ○ square

| Total Problems: | Total Correct: | Score: |

Name _____

Find the words from the word box in the word search puzzle below. Circle the words you find.

Sand Castles Word Search

```
S  P  C  T  O  W  E  R  E  P
A  A  O  L  T  G  B  T  C  Y
A  N  N  I  N  P  A  A  A  R
B  D  Q  D  N  R  B  X  S  A
U  O  U  B  O  T  F  I  T  M
C  A  Y  C  H  B  E  L  L  I
K  N  E  G  R  L  U  D  E  D
E  D  U  A  C  O  U  I  R  G
T  A  K  A  G  Q  G  V  L  Y
L  H  S  E  A  W  E  E  D  D
```

Word Box				
build	castle	laugh	pyramid	seaweed
bucket	decorate	pointed	sand	tower

Total Problems: Total Correct: Score:

Name _____

Name _____

Read the story below.

Saturday was always a special day for Dabney and her mom. Sometimes they would go to the park to play. Other times they would go for a walk. They couldn't do either of those things today because it was raining.

Dabney's mom had an idea. She wouldn't say where they were going. She wanted to keep it a surprise. Dabney was thrilled when her mom pulled into the train station. They paid the conductor for a one day train pass. What fun they had watching the rain as they rode through the city!

Fill in the circle beside the correct answer.

1. Who went to the train station with Dabney?
   - ○ her mom
   - ○ her brother
   - ○ her sister
   - ○ her dad

2. According to the story, what day was Dabney's special day with her mom ?
   - ○ Friday
   - ○ laundry day
   - ○ her mom's birthday
   - ○ Saturday

34 Total Problems: _____ Total Correct: _____ Score: _____

Complete the following activities. Write the answer on the lines provided where appropriate.

3. Why is Saturday a special day for Dabney and her mom?

_____

_____

_____

4. Why couldn't Dabney and her mom go play at the park?

_____

_____

_____

5. What was the surprise Dabney's mom had for Dabney?

_____

_____

_____

6. Use context clues to find the meaning of the following words.

thrilled _____

conductor _____

Name _____

Read the story below.

Luther wanted a trumpet. He listened to jazz musicians on the radio and wished he could play. He would play along with the radio pretending he had a trumpet.

One day Luther saw a trumpet in the window of a secondhand store. The cost was twelve dollars. Luther only had seven. Where would he get five more? Luther ran home and went to his room.

He knew his parents would not just give him the money, and thinking about it made him sad. He looked out the window and saw his neighbor, Mr. Thomas, bagging leaves. The bag kept falling over and he kept having to start again. "Mr. Thomas is having a worse day than I am," Luther thought, "He could use help."

Mr. Thomas was glad to have help. They finished quickly. Later that night Mr. Thomas knocked on the door. "Luther, I'm sorry I forgot to pay you," he said.

"I didn't expect any money," replied Luther.

"That's what made me even more grateful. This is for you." He handed Luther five dollars.

"Thank you!" said Luther. "This is exactly what I need to buy my trumpet."

36

Name _____

Complete the following activities. Write the answer on the lines provided where appropriate.

1. Number the sentences 1–4 in the order they happen in the story.

   _____ Mr. Thomas was having trouble bagging leaves.

   _____ Luther saw a trumpet in the store window.

   _____ Luther decided to help his neighbor.

   _____ Mr. Thomas gave Luther five dollars.

2. How did Luther get the rest of the money to buy the trumpet?

   _____

   _____

   _____

3. Why did Mr. Thomas give Luther money?

   _____

   _____

4. Why do you think Luther felt better after helping Mr. Thomas?

   _____

   _____

   _____

Total Problems:	Total Correct:	Score:

Read the story below.

Tonya and Isaiah were help-ing their aunt clean her ga-rage. She told Tonya and Isaiah that if they helped her clean out her garage, they could have anything they wanted from her junk pile.

They had been stacking old magazines and sweeping for over an hour. Tonya was starting to get discouraged. She didn't think that they were going to find anything that she and Isaiah could play with. Shortly after that, Isaiah called her over to the other side of the garage. "Tonya, look at these," Isaiah said. He was holding up a box full of different kinds of seeds.

"What kind do you think they are?" Tonya asked.

"I don't know," Isaiah said, "I would love to find out."

Tonya and Isaiah planted the seeds when they got home. They watered and weeded them for weeks. They watched the plants grow and they took care of them. As the plants grew, the children made predictions about what the seeds would turn out to be. After a few weeks they visited Aunt Lucille again. This time they had a gift for her: fresh vegetables from their vegetable garden!

38

Complete the following activities. Write the answer on the lines provided where appropriate.

1. Use context clues to find the meaning of the following words.

   discouraged _____

   predictions _____

2. Draw a line from each cause to the effect it had in the story.

   Cause

   Aunt Lucille had a messy garage.

   Isaiah and Tonya helped Aunt Lucille.

   Isaiah and Tonya took care of their garden.

   Effect

   They got to keep the seeds that they found.

   Aunt Lucille asked the kids to help clean her garage.

   Isaiah and Tonya gave Aunt Lucille fresh vegetables.

3. What did Tonya and Isaiah have to do to grow their vegetables?

   _____

   _____

   _____

Total Problems:	Total Correct:	Score:

Read the story below.

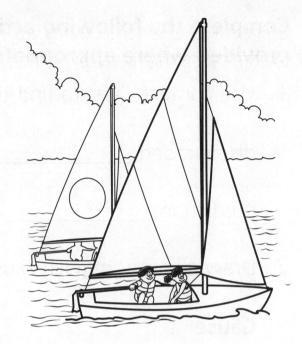

Spence and Kiesha had been getting ready all morning. They wanted to make sure everything was ready for the regatta. They washed the sailboat and loaded the life vests. It was time to go.

Mom and Dad watched as the sailboats sailed around the buoys. There was a lot of wind, so the boats were moving fast. "Look! Kiesha and Spence are in first place!" said Mom.

Dad picked up the binoculars to get a closer look. "They sure are!" said Dad. "I think they may win."

Kiesha and Spence took turns working the sails and steering. There were two boats just behind them. By working together, Kiesha and Spence won the race.

Mom and Dad ran to the edge of the water to meet Kiesha and Spence. "We are so proud of you," Mom said. "Working together helped you win the race."

Complete the following activities. Write the answer on the lines provided where appropriate.

1. What is the story mostly about?

_____

_____

_____

2. According to the story, what does the word "regatta" mean?

_____

3. What did Spence and Kiesha do to get ready for the race?

_____

_____

_____

4. What did Mom and Dad use to better see Spence and Kiesha?

_____

_____

5. How did working together help Spence and Kiesha win the race?

_____

_____

_____

Total Problems: Total Correct: Score:

Name _____

Read the story below.

Hoppy Spider was the eldest in his family. He had younger twin brothers who got attention because they were identical and a little sister who always got complimented on her beauty.

Hoppy wanted a talent that would set him apart from his brothers and sister. He entered the web-building competition held each year in his city. Every day he practiced building webs. When his friends and family asked him how he was, he smiled and waved, but he kept working.

The day of the contest, Hoppy was nervous and excited. He saw several spiders build strong webs. Then, it was Hoppy's turn. The referee blew the whistle and he began. Hoppy made his best web ever, and he did it in record time! The judges gave him a score of nine out of ten. That was the day's best score!

Hoppy's family crowded around him and his siblings asked if he would teach them how to build a good web. Other spiders in the town talked about the contest for months. Hoppy's dream had come true! He finally had a talent of his own.

Complete the following activities. Write the answer on the lines provided where appropriate.

1. Use context clues to find the meaning of the following words.

   identical _____

   complimented _____

   competition _____

   siblings _____

   nervous _____

2. What was Hoppy's problem?

   _____

   _____

3. How did Hoppy solve his problem?

   _____

   _____

4. Why did Hoppy practice building webs every day?

   _____

   _____

Total Problems:	Total Correct:	Score:

Read the story below.

Every summer Merrill went to camp. Every year she had a great time, but this year was different. Ruthie, Merrill's best friend, wasn't going. Ruthie was going to Maine with her family.

Merrill's parents dropped her off and she felt a tear on her cheek. She was already homesick, and camp had just begun. She decided to get her bunk ready. As she was tucking in her bedspread, she noticed a girl at the far end of the cabin. She looked sad. Merrill decided to go over and say hello. "Hi, I'm Merrill," she said.

"I'm Petra. This is my first year here. How about you?"

"This is my third year. It's a lot of fun. We go horse-back riding, hiking, swimming, and make great crafts."

Merrill and Petra helped each other set up their bunks. Then they went to meet the other kids by the trampoline. The girls took turns doing tricks on the trampoline.

By the end of the day the girls were good friends. Merrill wrote Ruthie a letter and told her she missed her. She also told her about Petra. She couldn't wait until next summer so Petra and Ruthie could meet at camp!

Complete the following activities. Write the answer on the lines provided where appropriate.

1. Read each phrase and decide which character from the story the phrase describes.

   went to Maine   _____

   has never been to camp before   _____

   has been to camp three years   _____

2. Why did Merrill cry when her parents left her at camp?

   _____

   _____

   _____

3. Find the word "bunk" in the story. What does it mean?

   _____

   _____

   _____

4. How did Merrill and Petra get over being homesick?

   _____

   _____

   _____

Read the story below.

 The Williams boys loved staying with Grandpa. Not only did he give the best hugs, but he told great stories. One thing they looked forward to on their visits was going out to breakfast. They went out to breakfast every time they spent the night. It was a tradition.

 The boys would get the same things off the breakfast bar every time. Harvey always got pancakes and bacon. Vince got scrambled eggs and sausage, and Henry chose toast, bacon, and strawberries. The boys loved the food, but it was almost more fun to choose what they wanted and get it themselves than it was to eat it!

Complete the following activities. Write the answer on the lines provided where appropriate.

I. On each boy's plate, draw what he had for breakfast.

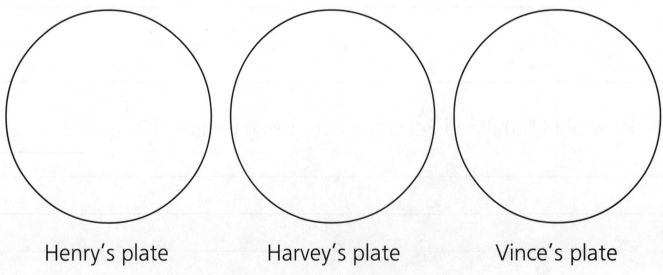

Henry's plate   Harvey's plate   Vince's plate

Total Problems:	Total Correct:	Score:

Complete the following activities. Write the answer on the lines provided or fill in the circle beside the correct answer where appropriate.

2. What are three things the boys enjoyed about staying with Grandpa?

_____

_____

_____

3. According to the story, what does the word "tradition" mean?

_____

_____

_____

4. What are some traditions in your family?

_____

_____

_____

5. When they stayed with Grandpa, the boys went to _____.
   ◯ lunch   ◯ dinner   ◯ breakfast

6. Who always got sausage for breakfast?
   ◯ Vince   ◯ Harvey   ◯ Henry

Total Problems:	Total Correct:	Score:

Name _____

Read the story below.

Al was a cat. He loved to be outside playing in the creek and catching mice. One day Al was trying to catch a mouse by the creek. He jumped over the creek and when he landed, his paw got caught between two rocks.

Al tried to get his paw out but it was starting to get sore. "Meow!" he cried, but no one heard him.

As the sun set, Al's family got worried. They looked everywhere for Al, but couldn't find him. Neighbors offered to help look for Al. They took flashlights and looked in bushes and trees. Al could hear their calls, but he couldn't move his leg. He was stuck. He meowed loudly, but still no one could hear him.

It got dark, and many of the neighbors went home. Al was frightened. He was afraid that no one would know where he was, and that he would have to spend the night all alone by the creek.

Finally, he heard footsteps coming. He saw a light and heard a voice. "I found him!" the voice said. "He's over here." Several people gathered around while the man who found him lifted the rock off of Al's paw.

Complete the following activities. Write the answer on the lines provided where appropriate.

1. What did Al like to do when he was outside?

_____

_____

_____

2. What was Al's problem?

_____

_____

_____

3. What did the neighbors do to help Al's family find Al?

_____

_____

_____

4. Read each sentence. If the sentence is a fact, write "fact." If the sentence is an opinion, write "opinion."

Cats are great pets.   _____

Al liked to chase mice.   _____

Dogs make better pets than cats.   _____

Read the story below.

There once was a bear who loved to eat honey so much that his friends began to call him Honey Bear. Honey Bear ran out of honey one day and decided to go out and look for more. All bears know to look for honey in trees, so that's just what Honey Bear did. He walked past the beans and peas that Farmer Jones had planted and tried to find a tree that looked like it might have honey in it.

Honey Bear looked and looked, but he did not see a good honey tree. He kept on walking. Finally, when he reached the edge of the forest, Honey Bear dropped down on one knee to rest. It was then that he saw the bee. Honey Bear remembered that bees make honey. So, Honey Bear let the bee lead him to his honey tree. There was more honey than Honey Bear had ever seen! He reached into the hive and filled up a jar with that delicious honey so that he could take some home to enjoy!

Complete the following activities. Write the answer on the lines provided where appropriate.

1. Why did Honey Bear's friends start calling him Honey Bear?

_____

_____

_____

2. What caused Honey Bear to remember that bees make honey?

_____

_____

3. Why didn't Honey Bear stop to eat peas or beans?

_____

_____

_____

4. Draw a line from each cause to the effect it had in the story.

Cause	Effect
Honey Bear was out of honey.	Honey Bear put honey in a jar.
Honey Bear wanted to take home honey to enjoy	He remembered that bees make honey.
Honey Bear saw a bee.	He went to look for honey.

Total Problems: Total Correct: Score:

Name _____

Read the story below.

Sally Squirrel loved to sing. Everyone could tell where Sally was because of her singing. She had a pretty voice, but she never sang the right words to songs. When Alex Owl asked Sally why she never sang the right words, Sally said, "I can't always remember the words, so I sing what I think sounds good."

"You can't make up words to someone else's songs," said Ollie Otter. "You have to sing the right words."

"He's right. You're bothering other animals," said Alex.

Several days went by, and no one heard Sally singing. "I miss Sally's voice," said Rita Raccoon.

"I do too. We hurt her feelings, and now that she's not singing we can't find her," said Ollie.

All of the animals looked for Sally. They tried every tree and burrow in the forest. Rita found Sally by the creek. "I thought I wouldn't bother anyone here," said Sally.

"We're sorry Sally. We miss your voice." said Rita.

On the way back Sally was quiet. Then, she began to sing a new song. The animals listened with tears in their eyes. It was a song about them. "I wrote it to thank you for being my friends," she said.

Complete the following activities. Write the answer on the lines provided where appropriate.

1. What was Sally's problem?

_____

_____

_____

2. Why did Sally run away?

_____

_____

3. How did Sally make up with her friends?

_____

_____

_____

4. Read each sentence. If it is something that could happen in real life, write "realistic." If it is something make believe, write "fantasy."

   A squirrel sings songs to her friends.   _____

   Someone makes up a new song.   _____

   A raccoon talks to a squirrel.   _____

   A friend tries to cheer up another friend. _____

Total Problems:	Total Correct:	Score:

Read the story below.

Maya and Sue were birds who were friends. When they were young, Sue's mom got a promotion at work, and her family had to move. Maya was so sad when Sue left, that after two weeks, Maya decided to travel west to find her. She waited until dark, and she sneaked away.

After an hour of flying, Maya grew tired. She stopped to rest on a limb. "Hello," said a voice from the darkness.

"Who's there?" asked Maya.

"It is I... O'Shay Owl. Where are you going so late at night, my young friend?"

"I'm going to see my friend Sue. Her mother got a better job and they had to move. It is a long flight, and I am very tired."

"I'm going west, too," said O'Shay. "I'll let you ride on my back if you give me food and rest when we arrive."

Maya agreed. When the two birds completed their journey, Sue's mother fed them and let them rest. Maya thanked O'Shay. "I'll never forget you," she said.

Complete the following activities. Write the answer on the lines provided where appropriate.

1. Why did Maya sneak away from home?

   _____

   _____

   _____

2. How did Maya complete her trip when she got tired?

   _____

   _____

3. What did Maya promise O'Shay in exchange for a ride?

   _____

   _____

   _____

4. Use context clues to find the meaning of the following words.

   promotion _____

   completed _____

   journey _____

   arrive _____

Total Problems:	Total Correct:	Score:

Name _____

Read the story below.

There was a little girl who did not like to write even though she was a great author. Once, the girl's brother took her story book to school. He asked his teacher to read a story to the class.

The class loved the story so much that they begged their teacher to read another. "I know," said the teacher, "Why don't you ask your sister to come and read her favorite story to us." The little boy didn't want to tell his teacher that he had taken his sister's story book without asking, so he went home to find his sister.

When the little boy got home, he walked to his sister's bedroom. He told his sister that he had taken her story book, and that the class liked her story. She started to cry. "I like coming up with the ideas," she told him, "but writing them down hurts my hand. If only I could keep my hand from hurting."

"I have an idea," said the little boy. "You can tell the stories to me, and I'll write them down." The idea worked, and the sibling team grew up to become famous children's book authors.

Complete the following activities. Write the answer on the lines provided where appropriate.

1. What was the reaction of the class to the stories?

   _____

   _____

   _____

2. Why did the little girl start to cry?

   _____

   _____

   _____

3. How did the brother and sister team solve their problem?

   _____

   _____

   _____

4. Read each sentence. If the sentence is a fact, write "fact." If the sentence is an opinion, write "opinion."

   The little girl cried too much.   _____

   The class liked the story.   _____

   Sisters should not write stories.   _____

Name _____

Read the story below.

Taylor was ready for his big soccer game. He practiced all week long. His coach told him not to be nervous, but Taylor couldn't help it. He had butterflies in his stomach. He couldn't wait to start the game.

The referee blew the whistle, and the game began. The other team made their way down the field right toward the goal. One boy passed the ball. Another boy kicked it. The ball was heading right for Taylor! Taylor jumped as high as he could, put his arms up, and pulled the ball out of the air. He caught it! Taylor kept the other team from scoring!

It was a good game. Taylor's team scored two times, and the other team never scored. Taylor beamed as he left the field. "You are a great goalie, Taylor," one of his teammates said.

"Thanks," said Taylor. He was already looking forward to next Saturday.

Complete the following activities. Write the answer on the lines provided where appropriate.

1. Find the word "goalie" in the story. What does a goalie do?

_____

_____

Total Problems: Total Correct: Score:

Complete the following activities. Write the answer on the lines provided where appropriate.

2. What does "butterflies in his stomach" mean in the story?

_____

_____

_____

3. Why was Taylor looking forward to next Saturday?

_____

_____

_____

4. If the sentence in the ball is a fact, color the ball red. If the sentence in the ball is an opinion, color the ball yellow.

Soccer is a fun sport.

Taylor caught the ball.

Taylor should practice more.

Name _____

Read the story below.

Jack and Liz were tired of play-ing inside. They had been at the beach for days and it had rained every day. One day Jack found a map of the island in the attic.

"Look at this, Liz," he said.

"What do you think that big X represents?" she asked.

"I don't know. Why don't we try to find out?"

The two of them put on their bathing suits and searched for their shovels and pails.

Since it had stopped raining, Mom said Jack and Liz could go out on the beach. They had their arms full of digging tools and the map. Mom laughed when they said they were going to find buried treasure.

Liz laid the map on the sand. "This is the Miller's house. Let's go there and follow the map to the X."

When they got to the X, they started to dig. They dug in the sand for thirty minutes and were about to give up when Liz hit something hard with her shovel. "I think I found it!" she yelled.

Liz pulled a tiny black box out of the sand. They ran back to Mom to show her. They couldn't wait to go back to the beach the next day and dig for more treasure.

Complete the following activities. Write the answer on the lines provided where appropriate.

1. Why were Jack and Liz tired of playing inside?

   _____

   _____

   _____

2. What did Jack find in the attic?

   _____

   _____

3. Draw a line from each cause to the effect it had in the story.

Cause	Effect
Liz and Jack followed the directions on the map.	Liz and Jack had to play inside.
It was raining.	Mom laughed.
It stopped raining.	Liz hit something hard with her shovel.
Liz dug in the sand.	They found the spot where the treasure was buried.
The kids told Mom they were looking for treasure.	Jack and Liz got to go outside.

Total Problems: Total Correct: Score:

Read the story below.

Linda's mom asked her to wash the dishes. Linda filled the sink with soapy water and placed the dishes in the sink. As Linda started washing the dishes, her favorite show came on the television. Linda turned to watch the show as she was washing the glasses. Linda dropped a glass on the floor. The glass broke. Linda looked on the floor and saw that it was her mother's favorite glass. Linda felt very sorry.

Fill in the circle beside the correct answer.

1. Linda wants to be_____ instead of washing the dishes.
   ○ playing outside
   ○ reading a book
   ○ watching a television show

2. Who asked Linda to wash the dishes?
   ○ her mom
   ○ her dad
   ○ her grandmother

3. What did Linda do first?
   ○ Linda put the dishes in the sink.
   ○ Linda broke a glass.
   ○ Linda filled the sink with water.

Total Problems: Total Correct: Score: © Carson-Dellosa CD-2201

Name _____

Find the words from the word box in the word search puzzle below. Circle the words you find.

Linda's Chores Word Search

```
W D D I S H E S M K
L A R P X T X E N C
F Q S O N G T I T H
W I X H P I S N M O
A R L D R P E Z Y R
T W Q O S S E E F E
E T V S X Q O D U S
R A A T L F J A F M
F L C V Q I A R P U
G A P B R O K E N Y
```

Word Box				
broken	dishes	favorite	sink	wash
chores	dropped	glass	soapy	water

Total Problems: _____   Total Correct: _____   Score: _____

63

Read the story below.

Mr. Boltz's class would gather every Friday to discuss problems and brainstorm ideas for improving their classroom. One Friday, Benjamin suggested that they get a class pet. He said it would go along with the animal unit they were studying and it would be fun to have a live pet in the classroom.

Every student had a suggestion of what kind of pet they should get. Eliza wanted a bird. Thurman thought a guinea pig would be a great pet. Trey wanted a snake. Jasmine suggested a tiger. Mr. Boltz interrupted and said it had to be a reasonable pet.

Finally, after a long discussion, the class took a vote. The majority of the class wanted a guinea pig. They decided to hold a bake sale to raise money to buy the guinea pig. One parent even donated a cage. After all the money from the sale was counted, Mr. Boltz announced that they had enough money to buy two guinea pigs!

Circle the letter beside the correct answer.

1. This story is mainly about _____.
   A. class meetings
   B. getting a class pet
   C. a guinea pig
   D. putting on a bake sale

2. Who suggested getting a guinea pig?
   A. Benjamin
   B. Trey
   C. Eliza
   D. Thurman

3. Which of the following is not a reasonable pet for a classroom?
   A. guinea pig
   B. bird
   C. tiger
   D. rabbit

4. Why did Benjamin suggest the class get a pet?
   A. He had always wanted one.
   B. Pets were on sale at the store.
   C. Pets are easy to take care of.
   D. They were studying about animals.

Name _____

Read the story below.

Everyone in Mrs. Rathburn's third grade class agreed that the best time of the day was recess. The boys would play kickball and the girls would run relays, except for Ali. Ali wanted to play kickball. Every day she went to the field and waited to get picked for a team. Every day Ali was the last person picked. None of the boys thought she was very good. They always made her stand in the outfield, where there wasn't much action. They also made Ali kick last. She didn't mind though, she just wanted to play.

One day the game was tied up and recess was almost over. Ali's team had two outs, and it was her turn to kick. "Oh great!" said the boys, "We're going to lose for sure." Ali ignored them and walked up to the plate. This was her opportunity to prove she could kick. The pitcher rolled the ball right over the plate. Ali kicked the ball as hard as she could. All of the boys stared in awe. They couldn't believe it. Ali had kicked the ball over the fence. That meant an automatic homerun! No one in the school had ever kicked a ball that far! Ali won the game! From then on Ali was always picked first in kickball.

Name _____

Complete the following activities. Circle the letter beside the correct answer where appropriate.

1. At the beginning of the story, why was Ali the last person picked?
   - A.   She came late.
   - B.   She was a girl.
   - C.   No one liked her.
   - D.   She liked being last.

2. What is meant by the word "awe" in the story?
   - A.   for a long time
   - B.   amusement
   - C.   amazement
   - D.   awful

3. Number the sentences 1–4 in the order they happen in the story.
   - _____ Ali kicked the ball over the fence.
   - _____ Ali was picked first.
   - _____ Ali was the last person picked for the kickball team.
   - _____ The kickball game was tied up.

4. Why did the boys start picking Ali first?
   - A. The teacher told them to.
   - B. She proved that she was a good player.
   - C. She gave them candy.
   - D. She was a straight "A" student.

5. What is the main idea of this story?
   - A. Girls and boys should not play sports together.
   - B. Girls are better kickball players than boys.
   - C. Boys are better kickball players than girls.
   - D. Girls can play sports just as well as boys.

Find the words from the word box in the word search puzzle below. Circle the words you find.

The Unlikely Hero Word Search

```
Z  H  T  H  O  M  E  R  U  N
P  P  I  T  C  H  E  R  H  E
K  R  R  E  C  E  S  S  E  D
X  I  O  W  R  B  U  R  L  C
A  R  C  V  K  O  G  E  S  H
C  E  B  K  E  A  I  F  A  O
T  M  H  P  B  F  G  Q  S  S
I  A  Q  O  T  A  S  U  L  E
O  R  U  U  D  M  L  K  W  N
N  K  O  F  W  Q  I  L  Z  D
```

Word Box				
action	chosen	kickball	pitcher	recess
agree	homerun	outfield	prove	remark

Total Problems: ___   Total Correct: ___   Score: ___

Read the story below.

My days begin in the early spring. I start as a bud high off the ground. As I grow bigger, I unfold to face the sky. Throughout the spring and summer I am bright green, but as autumn approaches, I begin to change. Sometimes I am yellow and orange, and sometimes I am bright red. Eventually I will turn brown and fall to the ground. What am I?

_____

Complete the following activities. Write the answer on the lines provided where appropriate.

1. Who is the narrator of the story?

_____

_____

2. Draw the narrator of the story in each box.

spring	summer	autumn

Name _____

Read the story below.

Many people are afraid of bats. This is mostly because most people do not know how interesting and helpful bats are. Bats are the only mammals that can fly. When bats are babies, their mothers take them for a ride by letting them cling to their fur while they fly.

Bats are nocturnal animals. They roost during the day while hanging upside down. At night they wake up to search for food.

Different bats eat different things. Some bats eat fruit or pollen from flowers, while other bats eat insects. Bats help people by eating the bugs, like mosquitoes, that often bite people.

Even though most bats have very good eyesight, they use echolocation to fly. They make very high squeaking sounds, which bounce off of objects in their path, and come back to them. When bats hear the echo, they know how close they are to an object. Most of the sounds they make are so high pitched that they cannot be heard by humans.

Complete the following activities. Write the answer on the lines provided where appropriate.

1. Read each sentence. If the sentence is true, write "T." If the sentence is false, write "F."

    _____ All bats have poor eyesight.

    _____ Bats are active at night.

    _____ Most mammals can fly.

    _____ Some bats eat insects.

2. Use context clues to find the meaning of the following words.

    nocturnal _____

    roost _____

3. How are bats different than all other mammals?

    _____

    _____

4. Why do bats wake up at night?

    _____

    _____

Total Problems:	Total Correct:	Score:

Read the story below.

A symphony is an orchestra concert. An orchestra is a group of musicians that play together. Many different instruments are played in an orchestra. They are grouped into families. The families are string, woodwind, percussion, and brass.

Violins, cellos, violas, and the bass make up the string family. The strings are the largest family in the orchestra. String musicians play their instruments by pulling a bow across the strings or by plucking, or quickly pulling, their strings.

A smaller part of the orchestra is the woodwind family. Some of the instruments in this family are the flute, clarinet, oboe, piccolo, and saxophone.

The percussion family gives an orchestra rhythm. Any instrument that is hit or struck is included in the percussion family. Some of these instruments are the drums, cymbals, triangle, and xylophone.

Some of the loudest instruments are in the brass family. The trumpet, French horn, and trombone are all in the brass family.

Complete the following activities. Write the answer on the lines provided where appropriate.

1. Which word from the story means the same as the given definition?

   a group of musicians that play together   _____

   a concert played by an orchestra   _____

   quickly pulling   _____

2. Decide whether each instrument belongs to the string, brass, percussion, or woodwind family.

   flute   _____   trumpet   _____

   French horn   _____   saxophone   _____

   clarinet   _____   violin   _____

   drums   _____   cello   _____

3. What is the largest instrument family in an orchestra?

   _____

4. Which family does an instrument belong in if it is hit or struck?

   _____

Read the story below.

Some turtles live to be over two hundred years old. Some scientists say that turtles, a distant relative of the dinosaur, are able to live so long because they take their time doing things. Turtles take a very long time to eat even the smallest amount of food. Turtles also take their time moving and growing. So remember that a turtle may be slow, but for a good reason.

Complete the following activities. Write the answer on the lines provided where appropriate.

1. What things take you a long time to do?

_____

_____

_____

2. What things do you do quickly?

_____

_____

_____

Total Problems: _____   Total Correct: _____   Score: _____

Complete the following activities. Write the answer on the lines provided where appropriate.

3. Read each sentence. If the sentence is true, write "T." If the sentence is false, write "F."

_____ Turtles never live over one hundred years.

_____ Turtles take their time when they eat.

_____ Turtles are related to dinosaurs.

_____ Turtles grow fast.

4. Why would moving and eating slowly affect how fast a turtle grows?

_____

_____

_____

5. What do you think would happen if a turtle began doing things faster?

_____

_____

_____

Read the story below.

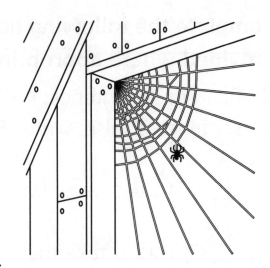

Many people think that spiders are insects, but they're not. An easy way to tell a spider from an insect is by looking at the legs. Spiders have eight legs and insects have six. Spiders also have two main body parts while insects have three.

Spiders can be helpful. They eat insects. This helps control the insect population. Some spiders build webs to catch insects. Others hunt their food.

Spiders can also be dangerous. Two extremely poisonous spiders in America include the black widow and the brown recluse. The black widow can be recognized by a red hourglass shape on its belly. The brown recluse is tan or brown and has a dark violin shape along its back. Unlike the widow, who lives in a web, the brown recluse makes its home near people. It likes dark, cool, and shady places.

Complete the following activities. Write the answer on the lines provided where appropriate.

1. Read each sentence. If the sentence is true, write "T." If the sentence is false, write "F."

   _____ Spiders are never dangerous.

   _____ Spiders are insects.

   _____ Spiders help control the insect population.

   _____ The brown recluse is a poisonous spider.

   _____ The black widow has a violin shape on its back.

   _____ Spiders have eight legs.

   _____ Spiders have three body parts.

2. Read each phrase. If the phrase tells about insects, draw a green line under it. If it tells about spiders, draw a blue line under it.

   have eight legs   have three body parts

   can be helpful to people   have two body parts

   build webs to catch food   have six legs

Find the words from the word box in the word search puzzle below. Circle the words you find.

Spiders Word Search

```
D D C A R E F U L S
R I P O I S O N U T
E Y F B P J R O N I
C S M F Z L R Q W I
L H L G E E N P I N
U A D W G R S S D S
S D F N L D E X O E
E Y A Y J G H N W C
V D E I G H T M C T
H O U R G L A S S E
```

Word Box

careful	difference	hourglass	poison	shady
dangerous	eight	insect	recluse	widow

Total Problems: ___ Total Correct: ___ Score: ___

Page 9

Name _____   Following Directions

Follow the directions for each picture.

answers will vary

pictures will vary

1. Draw a tail on the dog.
2. Draw black spots on the dog.
3. Make up a name for the dog and write it under the picture.
4. Give the dog a red collar.

1. Draw a large green circle in the box.
2. Draw three yellow triangles inside the circle.
3. Connect the three triangles with blue lines.
4. Trace the box with orange.

pictures will vary

pink

1. Draw a smile, a nose, and two green eyes in the circle.
2. Give the face curly red hair.
3. Draw freckles on the face.
4. Draw a blue box around the face.

1. Put an X on the smallest mouse.
2. Color the largest mouse pink.
3. Put dots under the two smallest mice.
4. Draw a line above the mice.

© Carson-Dellosa CD-2201   Total Problems: Total Correct: Score: 9

Page 10

Name _____   Following Directions

Follow the directions for each picture.

pictures will vary

red   blue   green

pictures will vary

1. Draw bows on the boxes.
2. Color the smallest box red.
3. Color the longest box blue.
4. Color the largest box green.

1. Draw a line from the top to the bottom of the circle.
2. Draw yellow and green stripes in the right half of the circle.
3. Draw purple spots on the left.
4. Draw red lines coming out of the circle.

pictures will vary

answers will vary

1. Draw a pig on the left side of the barn.
2. Color the barn red.
3. Draw two clouds and a sun in the sky.
4. Draw green grass on the ground.

1. Write your last name inside the box in black.
2. Trace the first letter with red.
3. Trace the last letter with blue.
4. Circle all of the vowels.

10   Total Problems: Total Correct: Score: © Carson-Dellosa CD-2201

Page 11

Name _____   Following Directions

Follow the directions to create the picture.

pictures will vary

1. Draw a picture of a house in the middle of the box.
2. Draw a little girl on the right side of the house and a little boy on the left side of the house.
3. Put a green bow in the little girl's hair.
4. Give the boy red shoes.
5. Draw a sun in the top left corner of the box.
6. Draw a sidewalk in front of the house.
7. Draw a dog beside the little boy.

© Carson-Dellosa CD-2201   Total Problems: Total Correct: Score: 11

Page 12

Name _____   Tina and Timmy

Read the story below.

Tina and Timmy are twins. They are eight years old. Tina and Timmy both have red hair, but Tina's hair is long and Timmy's hair is short. Tina wears her hair in braids. Both twins have freckles, but their eye color is different. Timmy's eyes are blue, and Tina's are green. Tina smiles a lot. She is missing her two front teeth. Timmy is not missing any teeth, but he just got braces. Tina and Timmy have a lot of similarities and differences.

Write the answer to the questions on the lines provided.

1. What is the main idea of the paragraph?
Tina and Timmy have a lot of similarities and differences.

2. What are some things that are the same about Tina and Timmy?
They both are twins, are eight years old, have red hair, and have freckles.

3. What are some things that are different about Tina and Timmy?
Tina's hair is long and Timmy's is short. Timmy's eyes are blue and Tina's are green. Tina is missing her two front teeth and Timmy has braces.

12   Total Problems: Total Correct: Score: © Carson-Dellosa CD-2201

Name _____ Tina and Timmy

Find the words from the word box in the word search puzzle below. Circle the words you find.

Tina and Timmy Word Search

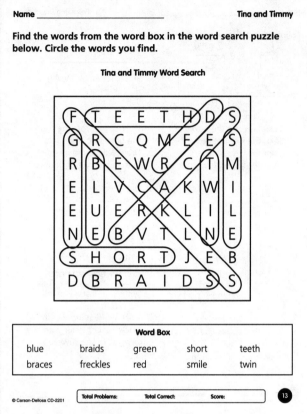

Word Box				
blue	braids	green	short	teeth
braces	freckles	red	smile	twin

© Carson-Dellosa CD-2201   Total Problems: Total Correct: Score: **13**

Name _____ Pizza for Dinner

Read the story below.

When Mom and Dad go out, Arden and Kate have a babysitter. The first time Chris babysat, the girls were nervous. "What if he isn't nice?" said Arden. "Don't worry," Mom said. "I'm sure he will be a great sitter."

When Chris got there the girls were playing checkers. "What do you want for dinner?" Chris asked. Both girls said, "Pizza!" at the same time. "What toppings do you like?" asked Chris. "I like pepperoni and mushrooms," said Kate. "I like green pepper and sausage," Arden said. Chris liked his pizza with plain cheese. "Looks like we have a problem," said Chris.

"I have an idea," Kate said. "Instead of ordering pizza, we could make one. That way we could put whatever toppings we want on our share." "What a good idea," said Arden. "Or, we could each make our own pizza." "You girls are smart," said Chris. The three of them went down to the kitchen and made pizzas for dinner. Before they knew it, Mom and Dad were home. "Did you have fun?" asked Dad. "Yes!" said Arden. "When can Chris babysit again?"

14   © Carson-Dellosa CD-2201

Name _____ Pizza for Dinner

Complete the following activities. Write the answer on the lines provided where appropriate.

1. What is the problem in the story?
   Everyone wanted a different kind of pizza.

2. How did Chris and the girls solve the problem?
   They each made their own pizza.

3. What are some other ways the problem could have been solved?
   answers will vary

4. Draw a picture of each person's pizza below.

Arden's Pizza *picture should include green pepper and sausage*

Kate's Pizza *picture should include pepperoni and mushrooms*

Chris' Pizza *picture should include cheese*

© Carson-Dellosa CD-2201   Total Problems: Total Correct: Score: **15**

Name _____ A Dog's Day

Read the story below.

Max loves to go to the park. If it is sunny outside Max's owner, Allison, takes him to the park after school. The first thing Max does when he gets to the park is chase the other dogs. After a fun game of chase, Max swims in the creek. Allison likes it when Max goes for a swim because it washes some of the dirt off of his white coat. Then, Max takes a nap under the picnic table before he and Allison go back home.

Complete the following activities. Write the answer on the lines provided where appropriate.

1. Number the sentences 1-3 in the order they happen in the story.
   _2_ Max goes for a swim.
   _1_ Max chases other dogs.
   _3_ Max takes a nap.

2. Color the bone that tells the main idea of the story green. Color the other bones blue.

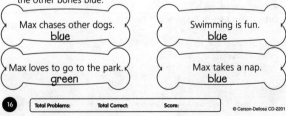

Max chases other dogs. blue   Swimming is fun. blue
Max loves to go to the park. green   Max takes a nap. blue

16   Total Problems: Total Correct: Score: © Carson-Dellosa CD-2201

80

© Carson-Dellosa CD-2201

Name _____ A Dog's Day

Find the words from the word box in the word search puzzle below. Circle the words you find.

A Dog's Day Word Search

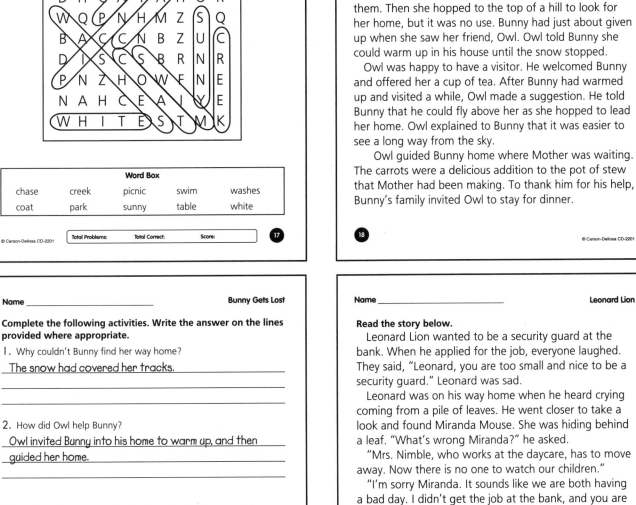

Word Box				
chase	creek	picnic	swim	washes
coat	park	sunny	table	white

© Carson-Dellosa CD-2201 | Total Problems: | Total Correct: | Score: | **17**

Name _____ Bunny Gets Lost

Read the story below.

Mother sent Bunny to the patch to gather carrots. Bunny picked them quickly because it had started snowing, and it was getting cold. She was on her way home from the carrot patch when she realized she was lost.

She tried to go back to the big oak tree to look for her tracks, but the snow had covered them. Then she hopped to the top of a hill to look for her home, but it was no use. Bunny had just about given up when she saw her friend, Owl. Owl told Bunny she could warm up in his house until the snow stopped.

Owl was happy to have a visitor. He welcomed Bunny and offered her a cup of tea. After Bunny had warmed up and visited a while, Owl made a suggestion. He told Bunny that he could fly above her as she hopped to lead her home. Owl explained to Bunny that it was easier to see a long way from the sky.

Owl guided Bunny home where Mother was waiting. The carrots were a delicious addition to the pot of stew that Mother had been making. To thank him for his help, Bunny's family invited Owl to stay for dinner.

18 © Carson-Dellosa CD-2201

Name _____ Bunny Gets Lost

Complete the following activities. Write the answer on the lines provided where appropriate.

1. Why couldn't Bunny find her way home?

   The snow had covered her tracks.

   _____

   _____

2. How did Owl help Bunny?

   Owl invited Bunny into his home to warm up, and then
   guided her home.

   _____

3. Number the sentences 1 – 5 in the order they happen in the story.

   2 Bunny realized that she was lost.

   1 Mother sent Bunny to the carrot patch to get carrots.

   4 Bunny and Owl had tea and visited.

   3 Bunny went back to the oak tree to look for her tracks.

   5 Owl joined Bunny's family for stew.

© Carson-Dellosa CD-2201 | Total Problems: | Total Correct: | Score: | **19**

Name _____ Leonard Lion

Read the story below.

Leonard Lion wanted to be a security guard at the bank. When he applied for the job, everyone laughed. They said, "Leonard, you are too small and nice to be a security guard." Leonard was sad.

Leonard was on his way home when he heard crying coming from a pile of leaves. He went closer to take a look and found Miranda Mouse. She was hiding behind a leaf. "What's wrong Miranda?" he asked.

"Mrs. Nimble, who works at the daycare, has to move away. Now there is no one to watch our children."

"I'm sorry Miranda. It sounds like we are both having a bad day. I didn't get the job at the bank, and you are worried about who will watch your children."

"I have an idea," said Miranda. "You are great with children, and it sounds like you need a job. What do you think about working at the daycare?"

"Well," said Leonard, "I'll try it and see how it goes."

Leonard loved working in the daycare, and the children loved Leonard. He read stories, gave out hugs, and painted with the children. Leonard never worried about not being big or tough again.

20 © Carson-Dellosa CD-2201

Name _____   Darby and the Inchworm

Complete the following activities. Write the answer on the lines provided where appropriate.

1. What was the inchworm's problem?

   The leaf the inchworm was on fell off the tree and it
   would take him all day to climb up the tree again.
   _____

2. Read each sentence. If it is something that could happen in real life, write "realistic." If it is something make believe, write "fantasy."

   Darby helps her father rake the yard.   _realistic_

   An inchworm talks to a little girl.   _fantasy_

   An inchworm falls from a tree.   _realistic_

   Dad takes a break for lunch.   _realistic_

3. Number the sentences 1–4 in the order they happen in the story.

   _3_ Darby helped the inchworm.

   _4_ Darby helped Dad finish raking the leaves.

   _2_ An inchworm said hello to Darby.

   _1_ Dad took a lunch break.

| Total Problems: | Total Correct: | Score: | **25** |

© Carson-Dellosa CD-2201

Name _____   Hank and Ruby

Read the story below.

Hank and Ruby were fish who lived in a pond. They loved to play tricks on other fish. Hank and Ruby liked to hide behind rocks and swim out in front of other fish to scare them.

The fish in the pond came up with a plan to teach Hank and Ruby a lesson. The fish met and swam closely together. By swimming that way, they looked like one enormous fish.

First they passed Ruby. She was hiding behind a plant waiting to scare someone. When she peeked out to see how close they were, Ruby was so frightened that she swam rapidly in the other direction.

Hank heard Ruby coming and thought that she was going to play a joke on him. He hid behind a rock and waited. When he heard her get closer, he jumped out. He came face to face with Ruby and with what looked like the world's largest fish! Hank and Ruby were terrified. They had never seen a fish so big. They swam away. Hank and Ruby were very careful from then on. No one ever told them that they had been tricked, but neither Hank nor Ruby tried to scare another fish again.

26

© Carson-Dellosa CD-2201

Name _____   Hank and Ruby

Complete the following activities. Write the answer on the lines provided where appropriate.

1. Who are the main characters in the story?
   Hank and Ruby

2. What is the setting of the story?
   a pond
   _____

3. How did Hank and Ruby scare the other fish?
   They would hide behind rocks and swim out in front
   of the other fish.

4. Why did Hank and Ruby stop scaring the other fish?
   The other fish scared them.
   _____

5. Use context clues to find the meaning of the following words.

   frighten   _to scare_

   terrified   _afraid or scared_

   enormous   _big_

   rapidly   _quickly_

   peeked   _looked_

| Total Problems: | Total Correct: | Score: | **27** |

© Carson-Dellosa CD-2201

Name _____   Camping

Read the story below.

John's scout group was going camping. He had a lot to do to get ready. He knew it was important to check his camping equipment to make sure everything worked. John laid his sleeping bag, tent, and cooking set on his bed, and his dad helped him inspect it.

Next, John went to the kitchen. John made trail mix in case he got hungry while hiking. He put peanuts, raisins, and chocolate chips in a plastic bag and shook it.

The next morning John's dad drove him to meet the other scouts. The leader helped them load their equipment into the truck. After driving an hour they arrived.

When they got there, everyone put on their backpacks and hiked toward the campsite. They stopped for a break after a while and had a snack. Everyone agreed that John's trail mix was delicious.

After their snack, the boys finished the hike to camp. When they arrived, they pitched their tents, collected firewood, and cleaned the campsite. The scout leader built a fire and they roasted hot dogs and marshmallows. They ended the day telling stories by the campfire.

28

© Carson-Dellosa CD-2201

Name _____   Camping

Complete the following activities. Write the answer on the lines provided where appropriate.

1. Number the sentences 1-4 in the order they happen in the story.

   __3__ John shared his trail mix.

   __1__ Dad drove John to meet the others.

   __4__ Stories were told by the campfire.

   __2__ The boys set up camp.

2. According to the story, how do you make trail mix?

   __Mix peanuts, raisins, and chocolate chips__

   __together in a bag.__

3. Which word from the story means the same as the given definition?

   checking to make sure something works __inspect__

   following a trail through the woods __hiking__

   spending the night in the woods __camping__

   putting up a tent __pitching__

© Carson-Dellosa CD-2201 | Total Problems: | Total Correct: | Score: | **29**

Name _____   Helena Horsefly and Señor Frog

Read the story below.

Helena Horsefly was a hard worker. She had never had a vacation. So, one day she decided to go to Mexico.

The first thing she did when she arrived was eat dinner. On her way out of the restaurant, she noticed that the man at the next table had forgotten his wallet. "I should return this," thought Helena. She took it to the address on the driver's license, which turned out to be a mansion. Helena knocked and waited. Finally, a handsome frog came to the door.

"I'm sorry to trouble you," Helena said, "but a man left his wallet where I was dining. This is the address on his license, so I thought I would return it. "

"That's my doorman Alfred's wallet," said the frog. "He is off tonight. I am Señor Frog."

"I am pleased to meet you," said Helena. Señor Frog invited Helena to come inside. After that night they spent a lot of time together and eventually fell in love. They decided to get married. Helena quit her job and moved to Mexico. She was so glad that she had decided to take a vacation.

30   © Carson-Dellosa CD-2201

Name _____   Helena Horsefly and Señor Frog

Complete the following activities. Write the answer on the lines provided where appropriate.

1. Why did Helena go to Señor Frog's house?

   __She wanted to return a wallet she found with his__

   __address inside.__

2. What happened when Helena got to Señor Frog's house?

   __She met him and found out that the wallet belonged__

   __to his doorman.__

3. Who is Alfred?

   __Señor Frog's doorman__

4. Number the sentences 1-4 in the order they happen in the story.

   __3__ Señor Frog introduced himself to Helena.

   __4__ Helena and Señor Frog got married.

   __1__ Helena went to Mexico.

   __2__ Helena found a wallet.

© Carson-Dellosa CD-2201 | Total Problems: | Total Correct: | Score: | **31**

Name _____   Sand Castles

Read the story below.

Latisha, Hope, and Valeria decided to build sand castles. Latisha made a castle by letting wet sand drip between her fingers. When she was finished, her castle had two pointed towers.

Hope used a bucket to make her castle. She put two buckets of sand side by side and put a third bucket on top. Her castle looked like a pyramid.

Valeria's castle was square. She collected shells and seaweed from the beach to decorate her castle. She used her fingers to add square windows on the sides.

All of the castles were beautiful. The girls laughed as the waves knocked down their castles. They knew that tomorrow they could build some new ones.

Fill in the circle beside the correct answer.

1. How many towers did Latisha's castle have?
   ○ four   ● two   ○ one

2. What did Hope's castle look like when it was finished?
   ● a pyramid   ○ a box   ○ a seashell

3. What was the shape of Valeria's castle?
   ○ circle   ○ triangle   ● square

32 | Total Problems: | Total Correct: | Score: | © Carson-Dellosa CD-2201

Name _____ Sand Castles

Find the words from the word box in the word search puzzle below. Circle the words you find.

Sand Castles Word Search

```
S P C T O W E R E P
A A O L T G B T C Y
A N N I N P A A A R
B D Q D N R B X S A
U O U B O T F I T M
C A Y C H B E L L I
K N E G R L U D E D
E D U A C O U I R G
T A K A G Q G V L Y
L H S E A W E E D D
```

Word Box				
build	castle	laugh	pyramid	seaweed
bucket	decorate	pointed	sand	tower

© Carson-Dellosa CD-2201   Total Problems: Total Correct: Score: **33**

Name _____ The Rainy Day

Read the story below.

Saturday was always a special day for Dabney and her mom. Sometimes they would go to the park to play. Other times they would go for a walk. They couldn't do either of those things today because it was raining.

Dabney's mom had an idea. She wouldn't say where they were going. She wanted to keep it a surprise. Dabney was thrilled when her mom pulled into the train station. They paid the conductor for a one day train pass. What fun they had watching the rain as they rode through the city!

Fill in the circle beside the correct answer.

1. Who went to the train station with Dabney?
   ● her mom   ○ her sister
   ○ her brother   ○ her dad

2. According to the story, what day was Dabney's special day with her mom ?
   ○ Friday   ○ her mom's birthday
   ○ laundry day   ● Saturday

34   Total Problems: Total Correct: Score: © Carson-Dellosa CD-2201

Name _____ The Rainy Day

Complete the following activities. Write the answer on the lines provided where appropriate.

3. Why is Saturday a special day for Dabney and her mom?
   They always did something fun together.
   _____
   _____

4. Why couldn't Dabney and her mom go play at the park?
   It was raining.
   _____
   _____

5. What was the surprise Dabney's mom had for Dabney?
   a train ride
   _____
   _____

6. Use context clues to find the meaning of the following words.
   thrilled _very excited_
   conductor _a person who collects train fares_

© Carson-Dellosa CD-2201   Total Problems: Total Correct: Score: **35**

Name _____ Luther's Trumpet

Read the story below.

Luther wanted a trumpet. He listened to jazz musicians on the radio and wished he could play. He would play along with the radio pretending he had a trumpet.

One day Luther saw a trumpet in the window of a secondhand store. The cost was twelve dollars. Luther only had seven. Where would he get five more? Luther ran home and went to his room.

He knew his parents would not just give him the money, and thinking about it made him sad. He looked out the window and saw his neighbor, Mr. Thomas, bagging leaves. The bag kept falling over and he kept having to start again. "Mr. Thomas is having a worse day than I am," Luther thought, "He could use help."

Mr. Thomas was glad to have help. They finished quickly. Later that night Mr. Thomas knocked on the door. "Luther, I'm sorry I forgot to pay you," he said.

"I didn't expect any money," replied Luther.

"That's what made me even more grateful. This is for you." He handed Luther five dollars.

"Thank you!" said Luther. "This is exactly what I need to buy my trumpet."

36   © Carson-Dellosa CD-2201

Name _____ Luther's Trumpet

Complete the following activities. Write the answer on the lines provided where appropriate.

1. Number the sentences 1–4 in the order they happen in the story.

_2_ Mr. Thomas was having trouble bagging leaves.

_1_ Luther saw a trumpet in the store window.

_3_ Luther decided to help his neighbor.

_4_ Mr. Thomas gave Luther five dollars.

2. How did Luther get the rest of the money to buy the trumpet?
 Mr. Thomas gave it to him.

3. Why did Mr. Thomas give Luther money?
 He was grateful for Luther's help raking the leaves.

4. Why do you think Luther felt better after helping Mr. Thomas?
 answers will vary

© Carson-Dellosa CD-2201 | Total Problems: | Total Correct: | Score: | **37**

Name _____ Mystery Seeds

Read the story below.

Tonya and Isaiah were helping their aunt clean her garage. She told Tonya and Isaiah that if they helped her clean out her garage, they could have anything they wanted from her junk pile.

They had been stacking old magazines and sweeping for over an hour. Tonya was starting to get discouraged. She didn't think that they were going to find anything that she and Isaiah could play with. Shortly after that, Isaiah called her over to the other side of the garage. "Tonya, look at these," Isaiah said. He was holding up a box full of different kinds of seeds.

"What kind do you think they are?" Tonya asked.

"I don't know," Isaiah said, "I would love to find out."

Tonya and Isaiah planted the seeds when they got home. They watered and weeded them for weeks. They watched the plants grow and they took care of them. As the plants grew, the children made predictions about what the seeds would turn out to be. After a few weeks they visited Aunt Lucille again. This time they had a gift for her: fresh vegetables from their vegetable garden!

38 © Carson-Dellosa CD-2201

Name _____ Mystery Seeds

Complete the following activities. Write the answer on the lines provided where appropriate.

1. Use context clues to find the meaning of the following words.

discouraged _frustrated or disappointed_

predictions _guesses about what will happen_

2. Draw a line from each cause to the effect it had in the story.

Cause
Aunt Lucille had a messy garage.

Isaiah and Tonya helped Aunt Lucille.

Isaiah and Tonya took care of their garden.

Effect
They got to keep the seeds that they found.

Aunt Lucille asked the kids to help clean her garage.

Isaiah and Tonya gave Aunt Lucille fresh vegetables.

3. What did Tonya and Isaiah have to do to grow their vegetables?
 plant the seeds, water the seeds, weed the garden, take care of the garden

© Carson-Dellosa CD-2201 | Total Problems: | Total Correct: | Score: | **39**

Name _____ The Regatta

Read the story below.

Spence and Kiesha had been getting ready all morning. They wanted to make sure everything was ready for the regatta. They washed the sailboat and loaded the life vests. It was time to go.

Mom and Dad watched as the sailboats sailed around the buoys. There was a lot of wind, so the boats were moving fast. "Look! Kiesha and Spence are in first place!" said Mom.

Dad picked up the binoculars to get a closer look. "They sure are!" said Dad. "I think they may win."

Kiesha and Spence took turns working the sails and steering. There were two boats just behind them. By working together, Kiesha and Spence won the race.

Mom and Dad ran to the edge of the water to meet Kiesha and Spence. "We are so proud of you," Mom said. "Working together helped you win the race."

40 © Carson-Dellosa CD-2201

86

© Carson-Dellosa CD-2201

Name _____ The Regatta

Complete the following activities. Write the answer on the lines provided where appropriate.

1. What is the story mostly about?

   Spence and Kiesha sailing in a regatta

   _____

2. According to the story, what does the word "regatta" mean?

   a sailing race

3. What did Spence and Kiesha do to get ready for the race?

   They washed the sailboat and loaded the life vests.

4. What did Mom and Dad use to better see Spence and Kiesha?

   binoculars

   _____

5. How did working together help Spence and Kiesha win the race?

   They took turns working the sails and steering the boat.

   _____

   _____

© Carson-Dellosa CD-2201 | Total Problems: | Total Correct: | Score: | **41**

Name _____ Hoppy Spider

Read the story below.

Hoppy Spider was the eldest in his family. He had younger twin brothers who got attention because they were identical and a little sister who always got complimented on her beauty.

Hoppy wanted a talent that would set him apart from his brothers and sister. He entered the web-building competition held each year in his city. Every day he practiced building webs. When his friends and family asked him how he was, he smiled and waved, but he kept working.

The day of the contest, Hoppy was nervous and excited. He saw several spiders build strong webs. Then, it was Hoppy's turn. The referee blew the whistle and he began. Hoppy made his best web ever, and he did it in record time! The judges gave him a score of nine out of ten. That was the day's best score!

Hoppy's family crowded around him and his siblings asked if he would teach them how to build a good web. Other spiders in the town talked about the contest for months. Hoppy's dream had come true! He finally had a talent of his own.

42

© Carson-Dellosa CD-2201

Name _____ Hoppy Spider

Complete the following activities. Write the answer on the lines provided where appropriate.

1. Use context clues to find the meaning of the following words.

   identical _look exactly the same_

   complimented _said something nice about someone_

   competition _a contest_

   siblings _brothers and sisters_

   nervous _jumpy or timid_

2. What was Hoppy's problem?

   He wanted a special talent.

   _____

3. How did Hoppy solve his problem?

   He entered a web building contest.

   _____

4. Why did Hoppy practice building webs every day?

   He wanted to win the contest.

   _____

© Carson-Dellosa CD-2201 | Total Problems: | Total Correct: | Score: | **43**

Name _____ Camp

Read the story below.

Every summer Merrill went to camp. Every year she had a great time, but this year was different. Ruthie, Merrill's best friend, wasn't going. Ruthie was going to Maine with her family.

Merrill's parents dropped her off and she felt a tear on her cheek. She was already homesick, and camp had just begun. She decided to get her bunk ready. As she was tucking in her bedspread, she noticed a girl at the far end of the cabin. She looked sad. Merrill decided to go over and say hello. "Hi, I'm Merrill," she said.

"I'm Petra. This is my first year here. How about you?"

"This is my third year. It's a lot of fun. We go horseback riding, hiking, swimming, and make great crafts."

Merrill and Petra helped each other set up their bunks. Then they went to meet the other kids by the trampoline. The girls took turns doing tricks on the trampoline.

By the end of the day the girls were good friends. Merrill wrote Ruthie a letter and told her she missed her. She also told her about Petra. She couldn't wait until next summer so Petra and Ruthie could meet at camp!

44

© Carson-Dellosa CD-2201

Name _____ Camp

Complete the following activities. Write the answer on the lines provided where appropriate.

1. Read each phrase and decide which character from the story the phrase describes.

   went to Maine   Ruthie

   has never been to camp before   Petra

   has been to camp three years   Merrill

2. Why did Merrill cry when her parents left her at camp?
   She was homesick.
   _____
   _____

3. Find the word "bunk" in the story. What does it mean?
   A bunk is a bed at camp.
   _____
   _____

4. How did Merrill and Petra get over being homesick?
   They became friends.
   _____
   _____

© Carson-Dellosa CD-2201 | Total Problems: | Total Correct: | Score: | 45

Name _____ Breakfast with Grandpa

Read the story below.

   The Williams boys loved staying with Grandpa. Not only did he give the best hugs, but he told great stories. One thing they looked forward to on their visits was going out to breakfast. They went out to breakfast every time they spent the night. It was a tradition.

   The boys would get the same things off the breakfast bar every time. Harvey always got pancakes and bacon. Vince got scrambled eggs and sausage, and Henry chose toast, bacon, and strawberries. The boys loved the food, but it was almost more fun to choose what they wanted and get it themselves than it was to eat it!

Complete the following activities. Write the answer on the lines provided where appropriate.

1. On each boy's plate, draw what he had for breakfast.

   picture should include toast, bacon, and strawberries.

   picture should include pancakes and bacon.

   picture should include scrambled eggs and sausage.

   Henry's plate   Harvey's plate   Vince's plate

46 | Total Problems: | Total Correct: | Score: | © Carson-Dellosa CD-2201

Name _____ Breakfast with Grandpa

Complete the following activities. Write the answer on the lines provided or fill in the circle beside the correct answer where appropriate.

2. What are three things the boys enjoyed about staying with Grandpa?
   He gave great hugs, told great stories, and took them
   out to breakfast.
   _____

3. According to the story, what does the word "tradition" mean?
   Something special you do at certain times.
   _____
   _____

4. What are some traditions in your family?
   answers will vary
   _____
   _____

5. When they stayed with Grandpa, the boys went to _____.
   ○ lunch   ○ dinner   ● breakfast

6. Who always got sausage for breakfast?
   ● Vince   ○ Harvey   ○ Henry

© Carson-Dellosa CD-2201 | Total Problems: | Total Correct: | Score: | 47

Name _____ Al

Read the story below.

   Al was a cat. He loved to be outside playing in the creek and catching mice. One day Al was trying to catch a mouse by the creek. He jumped over the creek and when he landed, his paw got caught between two rocks.

   Al tried to get his paw out but it was starting to get sore. "Meow!" he cried, but no one heard him.

   As the sun set, Al's family got worried. They looked everywhere for Al, but couldn't find him. Neighbors offered to help look for Al. They took flashlights and looked in bushes and trees. Al could hear their calls, but he couldn't move his leg. He was stuck. He meowed loudly, but still no one could hear him.

   It got dark, and many of the neighbors went home. Al was frightened. He was afraid that no one would know where he was, and that he would have to spend the night all alone by the creek.

   Finally, he heard footsteps coming. He saw a light and heard a voice. "I found him!" the voice said. "He's over here." Several people gathered around while the man who found him lifted the rock off of Al's paw.

48 | © Carson-Dellosa CD-2201

Name _____ Al

Complete the following activities. Write the answer on the lines provided where appropriate.

1. What did Al like to do when he was outside?

   Al liked to play in the creek and catch mice.

   _____

2. What was Al's problem?

   Al got his paw stuck between two rocks.

   _____

3. What did the neighbors do to help Al's family find Al?

   The neighbors used flashlights to look for Al in the bushes
   and trees.

   _____

4. Read each sentence. If the sentence is a fact, write "fact." If the sentence is an opinion, write "opinion."

   Cats are great pets.   opinion

   Al liked to chase mice.   fact

   Dogs make better pets than cats. opinion

Total Problems:	Total Correct:	Score:

49

Name _____ Honey Bear

Read the story below.

There once was a bear who loved to eat honey so much that his friends began to call him Honey Bear. Honey Bear ran out of honey one day and decided to go out and look for more. All bears know to look for honey in trees, so that's just what Honey Bear did. He walked past the beans and peas that Farmer Jones had planted and tried to find a tree that looked like it might have honey in it.

Honey Bear looked and looked, but he did not see a good honey tree. He kept on walking. Finally, when he reached the edge of the forest, Honey Bear dropped down on one knee to rest. It was then that he saw the bee. Honey Bear remembered that bees make honey. So, Honey Bear let the bee lead him to his honey tree. There was more honey than Honey Bear had ever seen! He reached into the hive and filled up a jar with that delicious honey so that he could take some home to enjoy!

50

© Carson-Dellosa CD-2201

Name _____ Honey Bear

Complete the following activities. Write the answer on the lines provided where appropriate.

1. Why did Honey Bear's friends start calling him Honey Bear?

   because he liked honey so much

   _____

2. What caused Honey Bear to remember that bees make honey?

   He saw a bee.

   _____

3. Why didn't Honey Bear stop to eat peas or beans?

   He was looking for a honey tree.

   _____

4. Draw a line from each cause to the effect it had in the story.

   Cause   **Effect**
   Honey Bear was out of honey.   Honey Bear put honey in a jar.

   Honey Bear wanted to take   He remembered that bees
   home honey to enjoy.   make honey.

   Honey Bear saw a bee.   He went to look for honey.

Total Problems:	Total Correct:	Score:

51

© Carson-Dellosa CD-2201

Name _____ Sally's Song

Read the story below.

Sally Squirrel loved to sing. Everyone could tell where Sally was because of her singing. She had a pretty voice, but she never sang the right words to songs. When Alex Owl asked Sally why she never sang the right words, Sally said, "I can't always remember the words, so I sing what I think sounds good."

"You can't make up words to someone else's songs," said Ollie Otter. "You have to sing the right words."

"He's right. You're bothering other animals," said Alex.

Several days went by, and no one heard Sally singing. "I miss Sally's voice," said Rita Raccoon.

"I do too. We hurt her feelings, and now that she's not singing we can't find her," said Ollie.

All of the animals looked for Sally. They tried every tree and burrow in the forest. Rita found Sally by the creek. "I thought I wouldn't bother anyone here," said Sally.

"We're sorry Sally. We miss your voice." said Rita.

On the way back Sally was quiet. Then, she began to sing a new song. The animals listened with tears in their eyes. It was a song about them. "I wrote it to thank you for being my friends," she said.

52

© Carson-Dellosa CD-2201

Name _____   Sally's Song

Complete the following activities. Write the answer on the lines provided where appropriate.

1. What was Sally's problem?
   She couldn't remember the words to songs. Her friends
   said Sally's singing bothered them.
   _____

2. Why did Sally run away?
   Her feelings were hurt.
   _____

3. How did Sally make up with her friends?
   She wrote a new song for them.
   _____
   _____

4. Read each sentence. If it is something that could happen in real life, write "realistic." If it is something make believe, write "fantasy."

   A squirrel sings songs to her friends.   _fantasy_

   Someone makes up a new song.   _realistic_

   A raccoon talks to a squirrel.   _fantasy_

   A friend tries to cheer up another friend.   _realistic_

© Carson-Dellosa CD-2201 | Total Problems: | Total Correct: | Score: | **53**

Name _____   Bird and Owl

Read the story below.

   Maya and Sue were birds who were friends. When they were young, Sue's mom got a promotion at work, and her family had to move. Maya was so sad when Sue left, that after two weeks, Maya decided to travel west to find her. She waited until dark, and she sneaked away.

   After an hour of flying, Maya grew tired. She stopped to rest on a limb. "Hello," said a voice from the darkness.

   "Who's there?" asked Maya.

   "It is I... O'Shay Owl. Where are you going so late at night, my young friend?"

   "I'm going to see my friend Sue. Her mother got a better job and they had to move. It is a long flight, and I am very tired."

   "I'm going west, too," said O'Shay. "I'll let you ride on my back if you give me food and rest when we arrive."

   Maya agreed. When the two birds completed their journey, Sue's mother fed them and let them rest. Maya thanked O'Shay. "I'll never forget you," she said.

54   © Carson-Dellosa CD-2201

Name _____   Bird and Owl

Complete the following activities. Write the answer on the lines provided where appropriate.

1. Why did Maya sneak away from home?
   She wanted to visit her friend Sue.
   _____

2. How did Maya complete her trip when she got tired?
   She rode on O'Shay Owl's back.
   _____

3. What did Maya promise O'Shay in exchange for a ride?
   Maya promised O'Shay food and rest when they arrived.
   _____
   _____

4. Use context clues to find the meaning of the following words.

   promotion   _a better job_

   completed   _finished_

   journey   _a trip_

   arrive   _get to a place you are going_

© Carson-Dellosa CD-2201 | Total Problems: | Total Correct: | Score: | **55**

Name _____   Sibling Stories

Read the story below.

   There was a little girl who did not like to write even though she was a great author. Once, the girl's brother took her story book to school. He asked his teacher to read a story to the class.

   The class loved the story so much that they begged their teacher to read another. "I know," said the teacher, "Why don't you ask your sister to come and read her favorite story to us." The little boy didn't want to tell his teacher that he had taken his sister's story book without asking, so he went home to find his sister.

   When the little boy got home, he walked to his sister's bedroom. He told his sister that he had taken her story book, and that the class liked her story. She started to cry. "I like coming up with the ideas," she told him, "but writing them down hurts my hand. If only I could keep my hand from hurting."

   "I have an idea," said the little boy. "You can tell the stories to me, and I'll write them down." The idea worked, and the sibling team grew up to become famous children's book authors.

56   © Carson-Dellosa CD-2201

Name _____   **Sibling Stories**

Complete the following activities. Write the answer on the lines provided where appropriate.

1. What was the reaction of the class to the stories?

   They liked the stories.

   _____

   _____

2. Why did the little girl start to cry?

   Writing the stories hurt her hand.

   _____

   _____

3. How did the brother and sister team solve their problem?

   The sister told the stories to her brother, and he wrote

   them down.

   _____

4. Read each sentence. If the sentence is a fact, write "fact." If the sentence is an opinion, write "opinion."

   The little girl cried too much.   opinion

   The class liked the story.   fact

   Sisters should not write stories.   opinion

© Carson-Dellosa CD-2201 | **Total Problems:** | **Total Correct:** | **Score:** | **57**

Name _____   **The Soccer Game**

Read the story below.

    Taylor was ready for his big soccer game. He practiced all week long. His coach told him not to be nervous, but Taylor couldn't help it. He had butterflies in his stomach. He couldn't wait to start the game.

    The referee blew the whistle, and the game began. The other team made their way down the field right toward the goal. One boy passed the ball. Another boy kicked it. The ball was heading right for Taylor! Taylor jumped as high as he could, put his arms up, and pulled the ball out of the air. He caught it! Taylor kept the other team from scoring!

    It was a good game. Taylor's team scored two times, and the other team never scored. Taylor beamed as he left the field. "You are a great goalie, Taylor," one of his teammates said.

    "Thanks," said Taylor. He was already looking forward to next Saturday.

Complete the following activities. Write the answer on the lines provided where appropriate.

1. Find the word "goalie" in the story. What does a goalie do?

   A goalie protects his or her team's goal and keeps the

   other team from scoring.

58 | **Total Problems:** | **Total Correct:** | **Score:** | © Carson-Dellosa CD-2201

Name _____   **The Soccer Game**

Complete the following activities. Write the answer on the lines provided where appropriate.

2. What does "butterflies in his stomach" mean in the story?

   It means that he was nervous or excited.

   _____

   _____

3. Why was Taylor looking forward to next Saturday?

   He played a good game and wanted to play again.

   _____

   _____

4. If the sentence in the ball is a fact, color the ball red. If the sentence in the ball is an opinion, color the ball yellow.

Soccer is a fun sport.   Taylor caught the ball.   Taylor should practice more.

yellow   red   yellow

© Carson-Dellosa CD-2201 | **Total Problems:** | **Total Correct:** | **Score:** | **59**

Name _____   **The Buried Treasure**

Read the story below.

    Jack and Liz were tired of playing inside. They had been at the beach for days and it had rained every day. One day Jack found a map of the island in the attic.

    "Look at this, Liz," he said.

    "What do you think that big X represents?" she asked.

    "I don't know. Why don't we try to find out?"

    The two of them put on their bathing suits and searched for their shovels and pails.

    Since it had stopped raining, Mom said Jack and Liz could go out on the beach. They had their arms full of digging tools and the map. Mom laughed when they said they were going to find buried treasure.

    Liz laid the map on the sand. "This is the Miller's house. Let's go there and follow the map to the X."

    When they got to the X, they started to dig. They dug in the sand for thirty minutes and were about to give up when Liz hit something hard with her shovel. "I think I found it!" she yelled.

    Liz pulled a tiny black box out of the sand. They ran back to Mom to show her. They couldn't wait to go back to the beach the next day and dig for more treasure.

60

© Carson-Dellosa CD-2201

Name _____   The Buried Treasure

Complete the following activities. Write the answer on the lines provided where appropriate.

1. Why were Jack and Liz tired of playing inside?
   It had been raining and they couldn't play outside.
   _____
   _____

2. What did Jack find in the attic?
   He found a treasure map of the island.
   _____

3. Draw a line from each cause to the effect it had in the story.

Cause	Effect
Liz and Jack followed the directions on the map.	Liz and Jack had to play inside.
It was raining.	Mom laughed.
It stopped raining.	Liz hit something hard with her shovel.
Liz dug in the sand.	They found the spot where the treasure was buried.
The kids told Mom they were looking for treasure.	Jack and Liz got to go outside.

© Carson-Dellosa CD-2201   Total Problems: Total Correct: Score: **61**

Name _____   Linda's Chores

Read the story below.

Linda's mom asked her to wash the dishes. Linda filled the sink with soapy water and placed the dishes in the sink. As Linda started washing the dishes, her favorite show came on the television. Linda turned to watch the show as she was washing the glasses. Linda dropped a glass on the floor. The glass broke. Linda looked on the floor and saw that it was her mother's favorite glass. Linda felt very sorry.

Fill in the circle beside the correct answer.

1. Linda wants to be_____ instead of washing the dishes.
   ○ playing outside
   ○ reading a book
   ● watching a television show

2. Who asked Linda to wash the dishes?
   ● her mom
   ○ her dad
   ○ her grandmother

3. What did Linda do first?
   ○ Linda put the dishes in the sink.
   ○ Linda broke a glass.
   ● Linda filled the sink with water.

62   Total Problems: Total Correct: Score: © Carson-Dellosa CD-2201

Name _____   Linda's Chores

Find the words from the word box in the word search puzzle below. Circle the words you find.

Linda's Chores Word Search

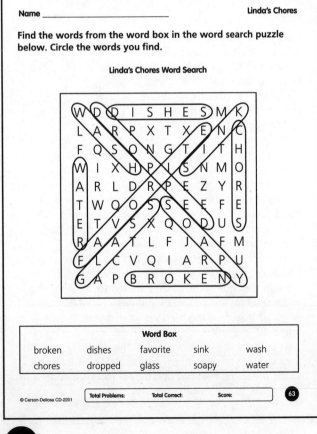

Word Box

broken	dishes	favorite	sink	wash
chores	dropped	glass	soapy	water

© Carson-Dellosa CD-2201   Total Problems: Total Correct: Score: **63**

Name _____   A Class Pet

Read the story below.

Mr. Boltz's class would gather every Friday to discuss problems and brainstorm ideas for improving their classroom. One Friday, Benjamin suggested that they get a class pet. He said it would go along with the animal unit they were studying and it would be fun to have a live pet in the classroom.

Every student had a suggestion of what kind of pet they should get. Eliza wanted a bird. Thurman thought a guinea pig would be a great pet. Trey wanted a snake. Jasmine suggested a tiger. Mr. Boltz interrupted and said it had to be a reasonable pet.

Finally, after a long discussion, the class took a vote. The majority of the class wanted a guinea pig. They decided to hold a bake sale to raise money to buy the guinea pig. One parent even donated a cage. After all the money from the sale was counted, Mr. Boltz announced that they had enough money to buy two guinea pigs!

64   © Carson-Dellosa CD-2201

Page 65

Name _____   A Class Pet

Circle the letter beside the correct answer.

1. This story is mainly about _____.
   A. class meetings
   B. getting a class pet
   C. a guinea pig
   D. putting on a bake sale

2. Who suggested getting a guinea pig?
   A. Benjamin
   B. Trey
   C. Eliza
   D. Thurman

3. Which of the following is not a reasonable pet for a classroom?
   A. guinea pig
   B. bird
   C. tiger
   D. rabbit

4. Why did Benjamin suggest the class get a pet?
   A. He had always wanted one.
   B. Pets were on sale at the store.
   C. Pets are easy to take care of.
   D. They were studying about animals.

© Carson-Dellosa CD-2201 | Total Problems: | Total Correct: | Score: | **65**

Page 66

Name _____   The Unlikely Hero

Read the story below.

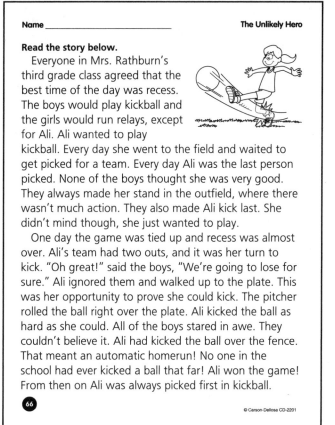

Everyone in Mrs. Rathburn's third grade class agreed that the best time of the day was recess. The boys would play kickball and the girls would run relays, except for Ali. Ali wanted to play kickball. Every day she went to the field and waited to get picked for a team. Every day Ali was the last person picked. None of the boys thought she was very good. They always made her stand in the outfield, where there wasn't much action. They also made Ali kick last. She didn't mind though, she just wanted to play.

One day the game was tied up and recess was almost over. Ali's team had two outs, and it was her turn to kick. "Oh great!" said the boys, "We're going to lose for sure." Ali ignored them and walked up to the plate. This was her opportunity to prove she could kick. The pitcher rolled the ball right over the plate. Ali kicked the ball as hard as she could. All of the boys stared in awe. They couldn't believe it. Ali had kicked the ball over the fence. That meant an automatic homerun! No one in the school had ever kicked a ball that far! Ali won the game! From then on Ali was always picked first in kickball.

66

© Carson-Dellosa CD-2201

Page 67

Name _____   The Unlikely Hero

Complete the following activities. Circle the letter beside the correct answer where appropriate.

1. At the beginning of the story, why was Ali the last person picked?
   A. She came late.   B. She was a girl.
   C. No one liked her.   D. She liked being last.

2. What is meant by the word "awe" in the story?
   A. for a long time   B. amusement
   C. amazement   D. awful

3. Number the sentences 1–4 in the order they happen in the story.
   _3_ Ali kicked the ball over the fence.
   _4_ Ali was picked first.
   _1_ Ali was the last person picked for the kickball team.
   _2_ The kickball game was tied up.

4. Why did the boys start picking Ali first?
   A. The teacher told them to.
   B. She proved that she was a good player.
   C. She gave them candy.
   D. She was a straight "A" student.

5. What is the main idea of this story?
   A. Girls and boys should not play sports together.
   B. Girls are better kickball players than boys.
   C. Boys are better kickball players than girls.
   D. Girls can play sports just as well as boys.

© Carson-Dellosa CD-2201 | Total Problems: | Total Correct: | Score: | **67**

Page 68

Name _____   The Unlikely Hero

Find the words from the word box in the word search puzzle below. Circle the words you find.

The Unlikely Hero Word Search

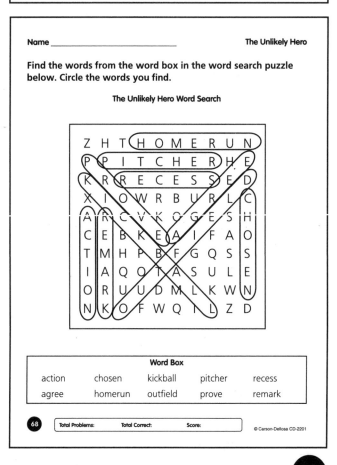

		Word Box		
action	chosen	kickball	pitcher	recess
agree	homerun	outfield	prove	remark

68 | Total Problems: | Total Correct: | Score: | © Carson-Dellosa CD-2201

Page 69

Name _____   What am I?

Read the story below.

My days begin in the early spring. I start as a bud high off the ground. As I grow bigger, I unfold to face the sky. Throughout the spring and summer I am bright green, but as autumn approaches, I begin to change. Sometimes I am yellow and orange, and sometimes I am bright red. Eventually I will turn brown and fall to the ground. What am I?

_____

Complete the following activities. Write the answer on the lines provided where appropriate.

1. Who is the narrator of the story?

   a leaf

   _____

2. Draw the narrator of the story in each box.

(bud on a tree branch)	(green leaf)	(yellow, orange, or red leaf)
spring	summer	autumn

© Carson-Dellosa CD-2201 | Total Problems: | Total Correct: | Score: | **69**

Page 70

Name _____   Bats

Read the story below.

Many people are afraid of bats. This is mostly because most people do not know how interesting and helpful bats are. Bats are the only mammals that can fly. When bats are babies, their mothers take them for a ride by letting them cling to their fur while they fly.

Bats are nocturnal animals. They roost during the day while hanging upside down. At night they wake up to search for food.

Different bats eat different things. Some bats eat fruit or pollen from flowers, while other bats eat insects. Bats help people by eating the bugs, like mosquitoes, that often bite people.

Even though most bats have very good eyesight, they use echolocation to fly. They make very high squeaking sounds, which bounce off of objects in their path, and come back to them. When bats hear the echo, they know how close they are to an object. Most of the sounds they make are so high pitched that they cannot be heard by humans.

70

© Carson-Dellosa CD-2201

Page 71

Name _____   Bats

Complete the following activities. Write the answer on the lines provided where appropriate.

1. Read each sentence. If the sentence is true, write "T." If the sentence is false, write "F."

   F All bats have poor eyesight.

   T Bats are active at night.

   F Most mammals can fly.

   T Some bats eat insects.

2. Use context clues to find the meaning of the following words.

   nocturnal awake and active at night

   roost rest or sleep

3. How are bats different than all other mammals?

   they can fly

   _____

4. Why do bats wake up at night?

   to search for food

© Carson-Dellosa CD-2201 | Total Problems: | Total Correct: | Score: | **71**

Page 72

Name _____   The Orchestra

Read the story below.

A symphony is an orchestra concert. An orchestra is a group of musicians that play together. Many different instruments are played in an orchestra. They are grouped into families. The families are string, woodwind, percussion, and brass.

Violins, cellos, violas, and the bass make up the string family. The strings are the largest family in the orchestra. String musicians play their instruments by pulling a bow across the strings or by plucking, or quickly pulling, their strings.

A smaller part of the orchestra is the woodwind family. Some of the instruments in this family are the flute, clarinet, oboe, piccolo, and saxophone.

The percussion family gives an orchestra rhythm. Any instrument that is hit or struck is included in the percussion family. Some of these instruments are the drums, cymbals, triangle, and xylophone.

Some of the loudest instruments are in the brass family. The trumpet, French horn, and trombone are all in the brass family.

72

© Carson-Dellosa CD-2201

Name _____   The Orchestra

Complete the following activities. Write the answer on the lines provided where appropriate.

1. Which word from the story means the same as the given definition?

   a group of musicians that play together _____orchestra_____

   a concert played by an orchestra _____symphony_____

   quickly pulling _____plucking_____

2. Decide whether each instrument belongs to the string, brass, percussion, or woodwind family.

   flute _____woodwind_____   trumpet _____brass_____

   French horn _____brass_____   saxophone _____woodwind_____

   clarinet _____woodwind_____   violin _____string_____

   drums _____percussion_____   cello _____string_____

3. What is the largest instrument family in an orchestra?
   _____string_____

4. Which family does an instrument belong in if it is hit or struck?
   _____percussion_____

| Total Problems: | Total Correct: | Score: | **73** |

© Carson-Dellosa CD-2201

Name _____   Slow and Steady

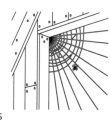

Read the story below.

   Some turtles live to be over two hundred years old. Some scientists say that turtles, a distant relative of the dinosaur, are able to live so long because they take their time doing things. Turtles take a very long time to eat even the smallest amount of food. Turtles also take their time moving and growing. So remember that a turtle may be slow, but for a good reason.

Complete the following activities. Write the answer on the lines provided where appropriate.

1. What things take you a long time to do?
   _____answers will vary_____
   _____
   _____

2. What things do you do quickly?
   _____answers will vary_____
   _____
   _____

| **74** | Total Problems: | Total Correct: | Score: |

© Carson-Dellosa CD-2201

Name _____   Slow and Steady

Complete the following activities. Write the answer on the lines provided where appropriate.

3. Read each sentence. If the sentence is true, write "T." If the sentence is false, write "F."

   __F__ Turtles never live over one hundred years.

   __T__ Turtles take their time when they eat.

   __T__ Turtles are related to dinosaurs.

   __F__ Turtles grow fast.

4. Why would moving and eating slowly affect how fast a turtle grows?
   _____answers will vary_____
   _____
   _____

5. What do you think would happen if a turtle began doing things faster?
   _____answers will vary_____
   _____
   _____

© Carson-Dellosa CD-2201 | Total Problems: | Total Correct: | Score: | **75** |

Name _____   Spiders

Read the story below.

   Many people think that spiders are insects, but they're not. An easy way to tell a spider from an insect is by looking at the legs. Spiders have eight legs and insects have six. Spiders also have two main body parts while insects have three.

   Spiders can be helpful. They eat insects. This helps control the insect population. Some spiders build webs to catch insects. Others hunt their food.

   Spiders can also be dangerous. Two extremely poisonous spiders in America include the black widow and the brown recluse. The black widow can be recognized by a red hourglass shape on its belly. The brown recluse is tan or brown and has a dark violin shape along its back. Unlike the widow, who lives in a web, the brown recluse makes its home near people. It likes dark, cool, and shady places.

76

© Carson-Dellosa CD-2201

Name _____   Spiders

Complete the following activities. Write the answer on the lines provided where appropriate.

1. Read each sentence. If the sentence is true, write "T." If the sentence is false, write "F."

    __F__ Spiders are never dangerous.

    __F__ Spiders are insects.

    __T__ Spiders help control the insect population.

    __T__ The brown recluse is a poisonous spider.

    __F__ The black widow has a violin shape on its back.

    __T__ Spiders have eight legs.

    __F__ Spiders have three body parts.

2. Read each phrase. If the phrase tells about insects, draw a green line under it. If it tells about spiders, draw a blue line under it.

    have eight legs
    (blue)

    have three body parts
    (green)

    can be helpful to people
    (blue and green)

    have two body parts
    (blue)

    build webs to catch food
    (blue)

    have six legs
    (green)

© Carson-Dellosa CD-2201   Total Problems: Total Correct: Score: **77**

Name _____   Spiders

Find the words from the word box in the word search puzzle below. Circle the words you find.

Spiders Word Search

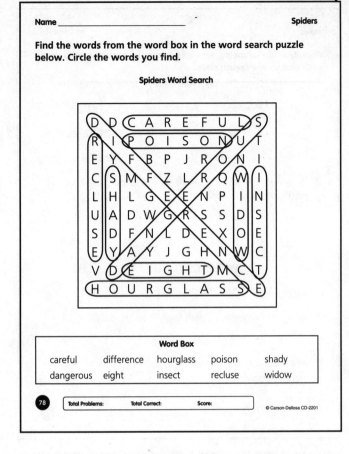

78   Total Problems: Total Correct: Score: © Carson-Dellosa CD-2201

Word Box				
careful	difference	hourglass	poison	shady
dangerous	eight	insect	recluse	widow